Controversies in Sociology
edited by
Professor T. B. Bottomore and
Professor M. J. Mulkay

18
The Knowledge Elite and the
Failure of Prophecy

Controversies in Sociology

The Knowledge Elite and the Failure of Prophecy

EVA ETZIONI-HALEVY

Reader in Sociology,
The Australian National University

London
GEORGE ALLEN & UNWIN
Boston   Sydney

George Allen & Unwin (Publishers) Ltd,
40 Museum Street, London WC1A 1LU, UK

George Allen & Unwin (Publishers) Ltd,
Park Lane, Hemel Hempstead, Herts HP2 4TE, UK

Allen & Unwin, Inc.,
Fifty Cross Street, Winchester, Mass 01890, USA

George Allen & Unwin Australia Pty Ltd,
8 Napier Street, North Sydney, NSW 2060, Australia

First published in 1985

British Library Cataloguing in Publication Data

Etzioni-Halevy, Eva
    The knowledge elite and the failure of prophecy.
– (Controversies in sociology; 18)
1. Intellectuals
I. Title   II. Series
305.5′52   HM213
ISBN 0-04-301192-6
ISBN 0-04-301193-4 Pbk

Library of Congress Cataloging in Publication Data

Etzioni-Halevy, Eva.
    The knowledge elite and the failure of prophecy.
(Controversies in sociology; 18)
Includes index.
1. Intellectuals. 2. Elite (Social sciences)
3. Social prediction. I. Title. II. Series.
HM213.E9 1985   305.5′52   85-13458
ISBN 0-04-301192-6 (alk. paper)
ISBN 0-04-301193-4 (pbk.: alk. paper)

Contents

Acknowledgements

This book on the Knowledge Elite marks a return to my first topic of interest in sociology, which I took up when I was still a student. I would like to take this opportunity to thank my erstwhile teacher Professor Joseph Ben-David, who first introduced me to this topic. I would also like to seek his indulgence if the present polemic is not precisely the result he was hoping for.

More recently, too, help has come from several eminent scholars. I would like to express my gratitude to Professor S. M. Lipset and Professor J. Higley for their most valuable comments on drafts of several of this book's chapters. I am also grateful to Professor Q. B. Gibson, Dr B. Martin, Professor P. Self, Dr B. K. Selinger and Dr G. Withers who have each read a draft chapter and who have made most helpful comments and suggestions. I owe a special debt of gratitude to the editors of the Controversies in Sociology series, Professor T. B. Bottomore and Professor M. J. Mulkay, and to my editor at George Allen & Unwin, Mr Gordon Smith, for their well-taken and constructive comments which have helped make this book a better one than it would otherwise have been. My deepest thanks go to Ms Mary Maxwell who volunteered to read the entire manuscript, who made extensive comments on both content and style and whose general encouragement has been invaluable to me. Subsequent revisions of the manuscript have been guided by all these comments, even though they probably did not do them justice.

Finally I hereby express my appreciation to Mrs Ann Illy for her adept research assistance and to Mrs Julie Myers and Mrs Zeta Hall for their assistance in typing and retyping the various drafts of the manuscript and for their unfailing patience in this thankless task.

EVA ETZIONI-HALEVY
Canberra
November 1984

Introduction

Almost thirty years ago Leon Festinger and two of his associates wrote a brief but instructive book entitled *When Prophecy Fails* (1956). In it they made the point that throughout Western history, people have periodically set themselves up as prophets in that (like the prophets of the Old Testament) they have reproved society for its wrongdoings, called on it to mend its ways and attempted to guide it towards a millennium. They have also marked themselves off as prophets in that they have made certain predictions on how and when this millennium is to eventuate. And when their prophecies have failed, this has frequently been followed by an even firmer conviction of their truthfulness. The failures have been rationalized away, new evidence has been looked for and existing evidence has been reinterpreted. All this has been done in order to legitimize the prophetic endeavour, that is, the prophecies themselves, the social movements which crystallized around them and the role of the prophets who led those movements.

The present book is about the Knowledge Elite, that is, intellectuals, the creators of knowledge and ideas[1] in modern Western[2] society. Its main thesis is that, metaphorically speaking, many Western intellectuals have also presented themselves as prophets. Like the prophets of antiquity and those analysed by Festinger *et al.*, they have done so by admonishing society for its shortcomings and by providing society with advice and guidance towards the future. Many of them are also very much in the business of prophesying (or forecasting, as it is more fashionably called) the future. In several respects their prophecy, too, has failed. Yet they, too, rationalize away their failures. And they still legitimize their intellectual endeavour by its prophetic qualities. That is to say, they continue to justify the creation of knowledge by its ostensible usefulness in guiding society towards a better future.

From this viewpoint, contemporary Western intellectuals are a remarkable group of people. Their means of production are their brains. Their capital is their education. The commodities they produce are knowledge, ideas and symbols. Their status and prestige rest on convincing others. And in this they have been so successful that many of their ranks have not only been able to set themselves up as prophets but have implicitly been accepted as such in Western society. Their influence has thus been substantial.

And yet Western intellectuals (a category to which, by profession, I myself belong), are prophets who have failed. They have failed not in the sense that the knowledge they provided has not been valid, nor in the sense that their advice has not been heeded by the powers that be. Rather, they have failed in that the knowledge they have provided and the advice they have proffered have not contributed as much as some of them have claimed to either the moral rectitude or the socio-economic well-being of Western society. They have failed in that their knowledge and advice has itself created problems for society.

Thus it is not that the intellectuals have not tried. And it is not that they have not been successful (in some cases) in having their ideas accepted and their knowledge implemented. It is merely that these ideas, to put it bluntly, have not always worked well. When their knowledge has been applied, and their ideas have been put to the test of actual practice and of the necessary ensuing compromises, they have frequently proved disappointing. Yet many intellectuals have continued to uphold the myth of the beneficial effect of their knowledge and ideas on society.

I claim that this is so because intellectuals in modern Western society are caught up in a structural paradox. Their subsistence, as well as their social position, depends on other people's willingness to finance their endeavour, and to a considerable extent on public funding. To obtain such funding intellectuals must convince the public that the knowledge they create is not merely of esoteric interest but has practical utility for society. To obtain such funding intellectuals are also under pressure actually to create the type of knowledge that has practical applications. But the more applied knowledge they create, the greater the chances that some of it will work to the detriment rather than to the benefit of society.

Part of the presumed utility of the intellectuals' endeavour lies in creating more of themselves through the process of higher education, from which many of their ranks derive their livelihood and institutional positions. But the more of themselves they create, the more the need for positions, the more funding becomes necessary, and hence the more they must convince the public of the usefulness of their knowledge.

This growing necessity for greater funding of the intellectual endeavour now coincides with a period of mounting socioeconomic problems – from which the knowledge-based advice and guidance proffered by intellectuals has not been able to extricate Western society. Also, with the recent economic setbacks (and for a variety of other reasons) there has been a squeeze on funding for universities and research. Because of this squeeze the need for intellectuals to convince society of the usefulness of their endeavour has become even more prominent. Hence, paradoxically, the Knowledge Elite has had to put the greatest emphasis on demonstrating the usefulness of its knowledge – in particular for the creation of policy – precisely when it has become most evident that those policies have not been working nearly as well as was previously expected.

Western intellectuals have failed as prophets also because their forecasts have frequently been off the mark. Those intellectuals who have set themselves up as forecasters of the future are following a longstanding tradition. This tradition harks back, if not to the Old Testament, at least to the founding fathers of the social sciences in the nineteenth century. Some of the giants of that century's social thought presumed to have discovered the trends of history and to be able to map its design for the future. Not surprisingly their prophecies were elegant failures.

Of these giants the most prominent, of course, was Karl Marx, whose predictions on the forthcoming demise of capitalism have not, so far, been realized. However, while Marx's prophecies may have misfired, they still bore the hallmarks of his greatness. For these predictions were based on the analysis of the presumed consequences of certain contradictions and conflicts, rather than on simple extrapolations of past or present trends into the future.

In contrast, the forecasts of present-day intellectuals have, as often as not, consisted of precisely such extrapolations. Periods of growing prosperity have frequently been interpreted as indicating even greater prosperity in the future. Periods of relative political quiescence have frequently been interpreted as a sign that Western capitalist society has learned to integrate and 'absorb' a variety of demands, and hence as indicating more quiescence in the future. It thus happened that some widely respected Western intellectuals foresaw a rosy future and failed to forecast the two most important socio-economic developments of the last decades: the student and New Left protests of the late 1960s, and the economic setbacks and ensuing social problems from the mid-1970s. Western intellectuals have thus been baffled not only by the present but by the future as well.

This argument can best be developed through a critique of the image *of* intellectuals sometimes invoked *by* intellectuals, in particular by the scholars who have recently focused their discussions on what they call the 'New Class' or the 'Knowledge Class' which includes what I here call intellectuals or the Knowledge Elite (see Chapter 1). These scholars have converged on the idea of the Knowledge Class (including intellectuals) as holding prominent positions in furthering the welfare of the 'post-industrial', 'technectronic' (or similarly termed), modern society. They have portrayed the Knowledge Class as a group of highly competent technocrats, who have produced ever more sophisticated systems of theory-based knowledge. They have claimed that these systems of knowledge have increasingly served as the basis of policy formation, that this has worked for the benefit of society, and that this benefit has increased especially in recent years. They have stressed that the Knowledge Class has thus helped guide society towards greater prosperity, more comprehensive services and a more equitable distribution of resources.

In contrast, I argue in this book that the creation of theory-based knowledge by intellectuals and the formation of social policy by politicians and bureaucrats are inherently disparate forms of human endeavour. I argue that the gap between them can be bridged only with great difficulty, that when theoretical knowledge is used as a basis of policy (or is in other ways applied for practical usage) the result is not necessarily beneficial for society. I further make the point that theory-based knowledge has not become more beneficial for society in recent years, but rather the opposite: benefits of knowledge for society have recently been levelling out; less felicitous effects have become more noticeable. Recently, knowledge-based policies have no longer helped guide society towards greater affluence, equality and freedom; they have even contributed to its mounting and increasingly intractable problems.

In fairness to the scholars of post-industrialism it must be said that they expressed their ideas mostly towards the end of the 1960s and the beginning of the 1970s when things were going well and were seemingly becoming better. They evidently supplied a fair assessment of developments in Western society and the role of intellectuals in it, up until then. But they presumed to do more than that, namely, to forecast the future as well. Indeed, the post-industrialists furnish a prime example of intellectuals summarizing existing trends and uncritically projecting them into the future. It is now clear that these projections were not a spectacular success. For no sooner were they published than they were rendered all but obsolete by the oncoming socio-economic crises they had so patently failed to foresee, and by the stunned helplessness of the (so-called) Knowledge Class in the face of those crises.

By now, in the mid-1980s, a new assessment of the socio-political role of intellectuals as part of that (so-called) Knowledge Class seems in order. For by now, the picture that emerges, far from being one of increasing social well-being, is closer to that of the sorcerer's apprentice who is no longer able to control the gush of events that threaten to overwhelm him. 'The waters rise. The apprentice rushes about with his bucket. The waters rise even faster. And none of us knows when, or whether, the magician will come home' (King, 1975, p. 286).

The confusion depicted here is first and foremost that of governments and their policy-making systems. But intellectuals (as part of the Knowledge Class) are implicated as well. In as much as many of them have been attempting to shape, and have actually been taking part in shaping, this policy-making and decision-making system, they (that is to say, we) cannot be exempted from shouldering a share of the blame. By the same token 'post-industrialists' are to blame for having greatly over-estimated the capabilities of these intellectuals. Both policy-oriented intellectuals and the post-industrialists who hallow their contribution thus furnish an example of prophecy that has failed.

PLAN OF THE BOOK

The first part of the book (Chapters 1–2) sets the scene by considering who intellectuals are and what their socio-political influence in Western society has been. It characterizes intellectuals as the Knowledge Elite and shows that they are sufficiently important and influential to make a critique of their socio-political role a worthwhile endeavour.

The second part of the book (Chapters 3–4) presents the main argument, outlined before, in greater detail. It shows that neither the intellectuals of the social sciences and humanities nor the natural and physical scientists (albeit for different reasons) have made the contribution to the welfare of society that many of them have claimed to make. It shows that both parts of the Knowledge Elite still continue to make that claim, on which the legitimacy of their position in society is now increasingly based.

The third part of the book (Chapters 5–6) illustrates this argument by presenting critiques of the socio-political roles of particular categories of intellectuals: economists, and natural and physical scientists concerned with medicine, warfare and production. The book concludes with an attempt to draw together the threads of the argument.

NOTES: INTRODUCTION

1   For an extension of this definition of intellectuals see Chapter 1.
2   This book is not concerned with a historical analysis, nor with non-Western intellectuals and societies.

Part One

SETTING THE SCENE

1

The Intellectuals as Knowledge Elite

Before the book's theses on intellectuals can be explicated, it is necessary, first, to establish who they refer to, or in other words, who are the intellectuals. Following Lipset and Dobson (1972, p. 137) and Brym (1980, p. 12), intellectuals are here defined as persons who are professionally engaged in the creation, elaboration and dissemination of theoretical knowledge, ideas and symbols. This would include the overlapping categories of members of university faculties (i.e. academics), scientists, social scientists, research scholars, journalists and writers. People who only, or chiefly, disseminate theoretical knowledge and ideas (such as schoolteachers) are not included. And neither are people who only, or chiefly, apply theoretical knowledge, such as engineers or medical practitioners. But people who both create and disseminate, or create and apply knowledge would be included. For instance, medical doctors or engineers who also engage in pertinent research would be seen as intellectuals according to this conception.[1]

The term 'intellectuals' first came into widespread use in France during the Dreyfus trial in 1894; it was used (mainly by those on the political right) to refer to men of letters who led the protest against the conduct of that trial. For some writers the term still suggests 'critical' or 'radical' thinkers. For many others, however, the concept has gradually come to be detached from its political connotation. For those it designates simply a category of people professionally engaged in the pursuit of knowledge and ideas. This is the sense in which the term is used in the present discussion.[2]

THE INTELLECTUALS AND THE KNOWLEDGE CLASS

According to this definition, the category of 'intellectuals' is a more narrow one than that of the 'Intelligentsia', or that which has recently come to be known as the 'New Class', or the 'Knowledge Class'. The term 'Intelligentsia' was coined in nineteenth-century Eastern and Central Europe and at the beginning it, too, referred to radical or revolutionary thinkers. Today, however, the term is used in Eastern Europe or communist bloc countries (and sometimes in the West as well) to refer to all people with higher education and/or to people whose higher education qualifies them for scientific, academic, professional, administrative, managerial and technological pursuits. Only part of those would qualify as intellectuals by the above definition.

The category of intellectuals is also more narrow than that of the 'New Class' or the 'Knowledge Class'. The term the 'New Class' has come into usage in America in the last fifteen years or so; it was introduced into scholarly parlance by people such as D. T. Bazelon, I. Kristol, P. D. Moynihan, N. Podhoretz (see Bruce-Briggs, ed., 1979); A. Gouldner (1979); and others. Like the term Intelligentsia, it has come to designate people with higher education engaged in intellectual, professional, techno-logical, administrative and managerial pursuits.

The term the 'Knowledge Class' for its part, has been introduced by, and has come to be associated mainly with, the proponents of the idea of the post-industrial society (or the post-industrialists) headed by D. Bell. It, too, designates basically the same category of people as the term Intelligentsia. Thus Bell (1973, p. 375) refers to the Knowledge Class as 'made up of four estates: the scientific, the technological, the administrative and the cultural'. The technological estate in turn includes engineers, economists and physicians (among others).

It is my argument that intellectuals (as here defined) ought to be clearly distinguished within the broader category of the Intelligentsia, the New Class, or the Knowledge Class, in order to highlight their distinctive social role and their peculiar social position. It is one of this book's major theses that the creation of (theoretical) knowledge, ideas and symbols is a distinctive form of human enterprise and that the application of that knowledge for the formation of policy, or in other ways, is exceedingly problematic (see Introduction and Chapter 3). Lumping the intellectuals whose main domain is the creation of knowledge together with administrators and managers, or engineers and other technologists whose domain is the application of knowledge, blurs the distinction between the two types of human enterprise. It thus leads to a distorted perception of the role of theoretical knowledge in society and of the role of intellectuals who create it.

Just as intellectuals have a distinctive social role so, too, do they hold a peculiar social position. Their position is special *in that they have much influence, but relatively little direct power over others*. Intellectuals are influential in the sense that they frequently succeed in convincing others of the validity and fruitfulness of the knowledge they provide. Also, they have an inordinate share in shaping the ideas that either legitimize or de-legitimize existing social and political structures. At the same time, intellectuals wield little direct power in the sense of being able to determine either the fate or the actions of large numbers of other people.

This is in contrast to other parts of what has been termed the Knowledge Class, in particular, administrators, who wield power directly on the basis of their positions in bureaucratic hierarchies. Intellectuals do not commonly hold such powerful institutional positions and if they do, they do so as administrators not as intellectuals. To the extent that intellectuals assume administrative duties in their respective institutions, they are apt to wield power over junior staff or students in those institutions. But this power is hardly comparable with that of top administrators, who may wield power not only over their own staff but over segments of society at large. For their institutional positions put them in charge of policies concerned with the allocation of resources on which these segments of society frequently depend (see Etzioni-Halevy, 1983a, ch. 7). And neither can the power of intellectuals compare with that of top managers in private enterprise, whose positions not only put them in charge of large numbers of workers, but also give them a leverage over government policies on which, once more, large segments of the population depend.

Lumping intellectuals into a single category with bureaucrats and managers thus blurs the distinction between influence based on knowledge and power based on institutional strongholds (though possibly backed up by knowledge), and creates the impression of intellectuals as more powerful than they actually are. Hence my intention of dealing with intellectuals separately and criticizing their own *distinctive* role in society.

ARE INTELLECTUALS A CLASS?

As intellectuals play a peculiar role and hold a special position in society, this raises the question of whether they also form a separate class. My reply would be that, contrary to what has sometimes been claimed (e.g. Brown, 1980), intellectuals do not form a class and, indeed, even the broader category of people referred to as the Intelligentsia, the New Class, or the Knowledge Class is not a class by any commonly accepted criteria.

Certainly this category of people cannot be regarded as a class on the basis of the Marxian criterion of relationship to the means of production. In this respect, Marx distinguished between those who own the means of production and exploit others and those who do not own and are exploited. In addition, he distinguished between those who 'command during the labour process in the name of capital' (Marx, [1867] 1976, p. 450) and those who do not (see Abercombie and Urry, 1983, p. 50). The so-called Knowledge Class cannot be distinguished as a separate class on the basis of either of those criteria. With respect to the first criterion: academics, researchers, administrators, or managers, as such, do not normally own their means of production. But this is a characteristic they share with the great majority of all members of modern society. Hence, it cannot serve to distinguish them as a class on their own. With respect to the second criterion the so-called Knowledge Class is divided: managers control the labour process of others in the name of capital; other parts of the Knowledge Class do not. Hence, this criterion, too, cannot serve to distinguish them as a class.

Perhaps it would be more feasible to regard the so-called New or Knowledge Class as a class in Weberian terms, namely, as a group of people with common economic life-chances. This is so, especially, since Weber distinguished the life-chances of different classes not only by property or lack thereof, but also (among the propertyless) on the basis of marketable qualifications based on training. What has been termed the New or Knowledge Class could thus be seen as a class by virtue of the very feature which distinguishes it from all other groups in society. Some contemporary scholars (such as Parkin, 1979; Konrád and Szelényi, 1979) have also made the point that the so-called Knowledge Class's (or the Intelligentsia's) specialized knowledge secures an advantage in economic life-chances for it. This group of people can also ensure a monopoly over the advantage by making the filling of a variety of positions dependent on higher education, diplomas and other credentials.

However, as Konrád and Szelényi point out, the Intelligentsia in Western society none the less does not constitute a class, because of the substantial internal differentiation within its ranks. It may be added that the qualifications possessed by members of this group differ widely in both their substance and marketability and hence in the economic life-chances they afford. Skills in fields that happen to be growth areas endow their owners with very good life-chances. Skills in other areas may have very limited marketability and provide their possessors with much poorer life-chances. Also, those knowledge-holders who occupy senior, permanent positions obviously have better life-chances than those who occupy junior or temporary positions, or who, as yet, have not been able to secure positions at all. Hence the so-called New Class or Knowledge Class may best not be regarded as a class with a commonality of life-chances but rather as a series of hierarchies, made up of people whose economic life-chances differ from almost the very best to almost the very poorest.

Ralf Dahrendorf (1959) has argued that in modern society classes are distinguished by power and authority. In a similar vein, Bell (1973, p. 361) defines a class as 'a system that has institutionalized the ground rules for acquiring, holding, and transferring differential power and its attendant privileges'.

And indeed he, and like-minded thinkers, single out the knowledge-holders as a separate and ascendant class on the basis of their presumed substantive power: 'In the post industrial society, technical skill becomes the base of and education the mode of access to power' (ibid., p. 358).

However, the comments made above with respect to the so-called Knowledge Class's life-chances are equally valid with respect to its power. Quite obviously some members of the Knowledge Class are much more powerful than others who might be their subordinates. Those, in turn, would wield more power than *their* subordinates. In other words, when power is used as a criterion for class, the so-called Knowledge Class does not emerge as a roughly homogeneous class at all, but rather (once more) as a series of hierarchies, that stretch from almost the top of the power structure to nearly its bottom.

Some Marxists, notably E. O. Wright *et al.* (1982), see managerial workers, professionals and experts as characterized by contradictory class locations in that they do not own the means of production but participate in their control or at least enjoy a considerable degree of self-control within the work process (contrary to proletarians who not only lack ownership of the means of production but also lack control of the labour process). However, as Marxist critics have already pointed out, Wright's theory is not greatly dissimilar to that of Dahrendorf, who views power or control as the decisive factor in determining class location. Therefore, what was said before regarding the hierarchical power structure of the Knowledge Class is relevant here as well. By Wright's criteria too, then, the Knowledge Class cannot be seen as a distinctive class in modern Western society.

If the so-called Knowledge Class is not a class, then this is the case, and even more so, with respect to intellectuals who form only part of this category of people. For intellectuals (like all other parts of the 'Knowledge Class') form hierarchies or ladders whose various rungs differ widely in economic life-chances and in the degree of their power. In these respects, for example, full professors (whatever they may be full of) differ greatly from tutors or assistants whose academic future is by no means assured. Certainly, then, intellectuals cannot be regarded as a class on the basis of the commonality of their life-chances or power nor, in fact, on any other basis.

THE INTELLECTUALS AS AN ELITE

If intellectuals are not a class what, then, are they? I suggest that intellectuals may best continue to be regarded as they have frequently been regarded before, namely, as an elite (see e.g. Bottomore, 1964; Eisenstadt, 1966; Broom and Selznick, 1977; and many others). Elites are here defined as minorities of people who are especially influential in shaping society's various institutional structures or spheres of activity. In modern society such structures and spheres include politics, administration, the economy, the military and the sphere of culture.[3] Accordingly one may speak of the political, the administrative, the business, the intellectual (cultural or knowledge) elites, and so forth.

The advantage of using the term elite rather than class to characterize intellectuals is that no commonality either of economic life-chances or of power or even of influence is implied. The term elite simply denotes a group of people who are inordinately influential in shaping some area of social life; by no means does it imply *equal* influence in that area. Indeed, as Suzanne Keller in the *International Encyclopaedia of the Social Sciences* has cogently pointed out, in all elites there are gradations of influence and this most definitely applies to intellectuals, that is, the Knowledge Elite.

As I have characterized intellectuals as an elite, or as a group of people inordinately influential in shaping one or more areas of social life, this still leaves me with the task of showing that intellectuals do, in fact, wield such influence. The next chapter is devoted to this task.

NOTES: CHAPTER 1

1   Some people, to be sure, while not intellectuals by profession, may well be intellectuals by personal inclination. Others, while intellectuals by profession, personally may have contributed nothing to the world of knowledge and ideas in their entire lives. But in a broad critique such as this one, these individual cases must necessarily be disregarded. It should be

noted that people who professionally engage in applied research would be included by this definition. Students, many (but not necessarily most) of whom are apprentices to the professional roles of intellectuals, are included in Brym's analysis but not in the present one.

2   This raises the question of whether all intellectuals are recipients of higher education. Scientists, academics, scholars and researchers evidently are. In principle, some journalists or writers might not be, but this is becoming a rather rare phenomenon.

3   Culture is here viewed in the broad sense as including not only literature, art and music, but all knowledge, symbols and ideas that form part of society's heritage.

2

How Intellectuals
Make a Difference

Why worry about intellectuals or the Knowledge Elite? Does
what they have to say make any difference? Or is theirs merely a
voice calling in the wilderness? In this chapter I will show that
intellectuals have recently exerted a substantial influence on
technology, production, policy, socio-political attitudes and
behaviour and thus, ultimately, on the socio-political developments of Western societies. I will show that not only has the
Knowledge Elite offered guidance to Western societies but that,
through several routes, its guidance has in fact been accepted by
these societies. *It is only because such guidance has been widely
accepted that it is worth performing the task which I have set for
the rest of this book: that of showing how and in what areas this
guidance has itself been misguided.*

ROUTES OF INFLUENCE

By definition, intellectuals are the ones who create, shape and
disseminate knowledge and ideas. There are several (overlapping) routes through which these sets of knowledge and ideas
influence patterns of socio-political action and thought in
Western societies.

The first and most obvious route is that of the control over
higher education. Through it intellectuals have a near-
monopoly over the selection, training and accreditation of their
own ranks and of other elites. For in modern society practically
all elites, including the educational, political, administrative,
business and industrial elites (not to mention the Knowledge
Elite itself), are increasingly recruited from among the
graduates of higher education. Intellectuals are thus in charge of

increasing numbers of potential elite members at the stage in their lives at which they are young and open-minded. Through their teaching and writing they not only help provide those future elites with the knowledge for the subsequent execution of their tasks but in the process unquestionably acquire a weighty share in moulding their outlooks on life. The members of these elites, in turn, then help shape and reshape society's basic educational, political and economic structures.

Thus, for instance, academics are in charge of the training and accreditation of the educational elites: both the decision-makers and the practitioners of education, that is, the actual educators. Educators, in their turn, are in charge of inculcating knowledge and ideas to youngsters many of whom will subsequently be influential in shaping society.

Academics in institutions of higher education also train, select and accredit the scientists, engineers, medical practitioners, computer experts and others who subsequently apply their academically acquired knowledge to such areas as production, medicine and warfare. There can be little doubt, and scholars from all schools of thought now agree, that science (and those who create and apply it) has become a leading force in the development of national economies. And as is also widely recognized, the ramifications of science – and scientists – as a force in the economy go far beyond production itself and create new conceptions and outlooks in society at large. And since government policy now, more than ever before, is also linked with economic production in many complex ways, the scientists who have a hand in the development of economic production also have an indirect route of influence on that policy. Science and scientists are also closely involved with the development of military technology and potential warfare, and (in connection with this) have a channel of influence on foreign policy.

Not only physical and natural scientists, but social scientists and experts in law, too, have indirect and direct routes of influence on economic production and both domestic and foreign policy. Graduates in economics, business administration and (to a lesser extent) other social sciences and in law increasingly have been occupying key positions in private enterprise. Law and social science graduates have also been assuming prominent positions in various sections of government bureaucracies. All these graduates have thus been serving as mediators between their teachers, the intellectuals (and the knowledge acquired from them), and concrete production, economic, welfare and foreign policies.

In addition, prominent intellectuals (especially university professors) are sometimes appointed to government positions (either permanently or temporarily) or else are engaged by governments in various consultantships, commissions of inquiry, committees, or councils in their areas of expertise. In all these capacities they provide an even more direct link between theoretical knowledge and government policy. Yet another route of influence by the Knowledge Elite on government policy is that of participation in applied or policy research commissioned by influential public institutions such as governments.

There have been additional routes to the intellectuals' influence on politics and society.[1] But rather than moving on to those, it is worth giving some concrete examples of the manner in which intellectuals have utilized one major route of influence: that of access to policy formation. The most prominent example is unquestionably to be found in the United States.

INTELLECTUALS AND POLICY: THE UNITED STATES

Despite a longstanding anti-intellectual tradition, American intellectuals have become quite prominent in policy-making structures in recent years. During the first 150 years of the Republic's existence intellectuals were not commonly found in government. Some initial changes in this occurred at the beginning of the twentieth century, but the breakthrough came during the Great Depression and the New Deal era. At that time significant numbers of intellectuals were brought into government, to devise policies for the alleviation of unemployment and poverty, and their numbers have been growing almost continuously ever since. The Second World War produced a vast proliferation of new agencies which 'swallowed up thousands of . . . intellectuals' (Draper, 1977, p. 51), and the penetration of policy-making bodies by intellectuals became even more noticeable in the postwar era. Many intellectuals who had been engaged by government agencies during the war retained an active relationship with the government after the war and many new roles for intellectuals were created. Especially prominent were the new roles for intellectuals in the State Department:

> A new breed of politicised intellectuals appeared – the foreign affairs intellectuals. What had been a fairly small field became a minor industry with branches in international politics, international economics, international arms proliferation and control, foreign aid, area specialisation and the like . . . If anything more were needed to reinvigorate the War-time and post-War boom in the procreation, care and feeding of politicised intellectuals, the Truman Doctrine of 1947 and the Marshall Plan of 1948 came just in time. They enabled large numbers of American intellectuals to fan out all over the world at government expense, scattering their largesse and advice far and wide. (Draper, 1977, p. 51).

At the same time the older roles for intellectuals in government became more prominent. In the Federal Reserve system, which itself became more influential in shaping the economy, academically trained economists (who retained intimate relations with their colleagues in academia) became more numerous and visible. At that time a closer link was also established between research organizations and the various government agencies. 'High officials turned repeatedly and frequently to the universities for assistance, enlightenment, counsel, guidance and personnel' (Shils, 1972, p. 174). In addition, private organizations (like the RAND corporation) performed research on contract for the military and the government on matters at the very centre of military and civilian policy.

Despite the advent of McCarthyism, these practices were not reduced by the Republican administration of President Eisenhower. According to Draper, some intellectuals felt that they were not really appreciated by the administration. But on the whole both the numbers and the status of university professors rose spectacularly during the Eisenhower period. Under the Kennedy administration the incorporation of intellectuals continued in an especially dramatic way, as Kennedy appointed to important posts a higher proportion of academics than any other president in history. Kennedy's closest aide, T. S. Sorensen, boasted that

> Kennedy's appointees had written more books than the President – a fast reader . . . could read in a four year term. One dreads to think how long it would have taken a President like Eisenhower to read the same number of books . . . It may be said without exaggeration that professors, ex-professors, and would-be professors were all over Washington – in the White House, in the bureaucracy, in Congress and congressional staffs, in almost all levels of government. (Draper, 1977, p. 53)

Under Lyndon Johnson many intellectuals were kept on, and contributed much during his first two years of domestic reforms, but Johnson's style and especially his growing involvement in the Vietnam war antagonized them and many eventually left. Richard Nixon tended to give fewer jobs to intellectuals, but under Jimmy Carter intellectuals were reinstated once again and appointed to some of the highest government positions in Washington.

All in all, despite ups and downs, the Knowledge Elite has been faring well in American government in recent years. This is attested to by, among others, L. J. Sharpe (1977, p. 43) who writes that 'each régime in Washington imports its own close advisers – the "in-and-outers" – and they usually include a strong leavening of academics'. With respect to social scientists, in particular, this is also attested to by P. U. Uliassi (1971, p. 309) who writes that they

> have been favored by official patronage on a scale unimagined only a generation ago . . . and encouraged – although little encouragement is needed in most cases – to

minister to the needs of officials in Washington who, as the collective modern prince, obviously require all the enlightenment that reason, in its modern dress, can offer.

For social scientists and other intellectuals, access to policy formation takes the form not only of appointment to political and administrative posts, but also of consultantships. Thus S. M. Lipset (1982, p. 150) reports on the basis of a survey of top academics (those 2,500 American professors who are members of major academies or honorific societies) that one-fourth had advised either the president or cabinet and sub-cabinet officers or both, and over two-thirds had served as consultants to government agencies.

Besides government consultantships, American intellectuals have acquired access to the making of government policy through a growing variety of academic and non-academic research institutes, including the aforementioned RAND corporation, the Brookings Institution in Washington, the Research Institute on International Change at Columbia University and several others. Non-academic research institutes in particular have proliferated to numbers and varieties unknown in the post-Second World War years, and they have become important performers of research directly related to government policy in the areas of domestic and foreign affairs and national security.

The research performed by these institutes is frequently financed by government agencies. In recent years the outlays for such research have grown phenomenally. With respect to social science research, for instance, federal outlays stood at US$6 million annually in 1951, but increased to US$421 million in 1971 (Useem, 1976, p. 613), and since then the 'river of research gold that flows from Washington', as Uliassi (1971, p. 313) calls it, has grown further. According to Rossi (1980), estimates of the amounts spent in the federal budgets of the last few years on applied social research vary from US$1 to US$2 billion per annum, and this does not include state and local government support. This is so even though the recent recession has brought about a funding crisis and large fluctuations in the project marketplace.

INTELLECTUALS AND POLICY: SOME OTHER WESTERN
COUNTRIES

The growing access of intellectuals to the policy-shaping process (though most pronounced in the United States) is not, of course, a uniquely American phenomenon. In countries such as Great Britain and Australia senior intellectuals, in particular academics, sometimes become involved in policy-setting through membership of commissions of inquiry or leadership of quasi-governmental agencies. According to Sharpe (1977), there has lately been a strengthening of the social science input into the activities of British Royal Commissions. In some commissions a social scientist has actually been designated as a research director who has undertaken or commissioned extensive research (the Donovan Commission on trade unions and the Redcliffe-Maud Commission on local government are prominent examples). In other commissions the social scientist member of the commission has undertaken such a role unofficially (the Seebohm Committee on personal social services, the Fulton Commission on the civil service and the Kilbrandon Commission on the constitution, for instance).

The American practice of the government commissioning studies from independent research institutes is also being introduced in Britain. According to *The Economist* (10 September 1983, p. 25), the British Treasury is considering the commissioning of studies (for instance, on the restructuring of health spending, national insurance and entitlements to unemployment and other benefits) from various research institutes.

In addition, as Sharpe (1977) reports, intellectuals are sometimes incorporated into the leadership of political parties or commissioned to do policy research for them. 'In the case of the Labour party, the cadre tends in fact to include a high proportion of ex-social science and history academics, or academic manqués' (p. 42). For its part the Conservative Party has some research institutes attached or related to it, including the Centre for Policy Studies and the Institute of Economic Affairs. In this manner intellectuals have become attached to both major political parties, thus invariably having access to both the critics and the makers of government policy.

There seems to have been some suspicion of social scientists among British policy-makers, but there are some indications that this attitude may be changing. The creation in 1970 of the Central Policy Review Staff, which advises the Cabinet, and the setting up in 1974 of an advisory team of social scientists in the Prime Minister's private office are some reflections of this change. So, too, is the creation in 1968 of the Civil Service College which maintains a social science-based research programme. The expansion of departmental research budgets is another indicator. In addition, a few academics (Bowden, Balogh, Kalder and Crowther-Hunt) have even been appointed to minor ministerial posts in recent years and one (Sir Claus Moser) was appointed to a senior civil service post as director of the Central Statistical Office.

In Australia, where basically the British political tradition is followed, a similar situation prevails. Intellectuals sometimes staff commissions of inquiry and occasionally are called in from academia as advisers to politicians or to fill senior bureaucratic posts (the participation of academics in the think tank put up by former prime minister M. Fraser and known as 'Policy Directions' is a prominent example). In addition, the Melbourne Institute of Applied Economic and Social Research acts as a kind of think tank for the Labor Party in the state of Victoria.

This phenomenon is even more developed in continental Europe where much policy research is done within, or on behalf of, political parties. In Germany, for instance, both major parties have formidable research institutes attached to them. And in the Scandinavian countries there are research divisions (run by social scientists) within party headquarters.

THE IMPACT OF INTELLECTUALS ON GOVERNMENT POLICY

So far, the routes of influence and the manner in which they have afforded intellectuals access to the policy-making structures in some Western countries have been reviewed. All this tells us little, however, about the actual results of that access, about the influence the advice and research results furnished by intellectuals have had on government policy.

Robert Merton once wrote that the honeymoon of intellectuals with policy-makers is often nasty, brutish and short. According to some observers, even after the honeymoon is over the results of that marriage are not substantial. Intellectuals present advice but politicians, not intellectuals, make decisions. In Draper's (1977, p. 57) words, 'Intellectuals propose; politicians dispose'. Moreover, 'To be successful, the intellectual must often propose just what the politician wants him to propose'.

The validity of this statement, at least in some cases, is well illustrated by an anecdote about the relationship that reportedly developed between one of Israel's past prime ministers, Levy Eshkol, and his scientific advisers, in connection with the proposed construction of a major power station. Under heavy pressure from the powerful Electricity Commission, Eshkol favoured construction of the station within the Tel-Aviv metropolitan area. However, he had to face a hostile public opinion, on account of the inevitably resulting pollution, by which over a million inhabitants would be affected. The solution he hit upon was to call in an expert from abroad for consultation. The expert advised locating the station well outside the city, whereupon he called in another expert, with similar results. Reportedly, he then called another one and another one, and so forth, until he had consulted twelve experts who all thought the station ought to be located outside the metropolitan area. He then sent for a thirteenth expert who counselled constructing the station within the city. Eshkol promptly accepted his advice and the station was built accordingly.

None the less, such an occurrence does not represent the only possible relationship between intellectuals and policy-makers. According to several observers, the role of intellectuals in government (somewhat like that of bureaucrats) is to furnish knowledge-based advice on the available options for policy decisions. This in itself is an important contribution to policy formation. For defining some options *ipso facto* rules out many others, and thus puts constraints on the decision-making process. Moreover, when the politicians themselves are undecided, the intellectuals' advice may well tip the scales.

This is not to say that the policy that is eventually

implemented necessarily reflects the intellectual's own vision. Before being put into practice the intellectual's input into policy proposals must necessarily face the ordeal of various pressures and counter-pressures (perhaps even by other intellectuals) so that the end result probably represents a compromise rather than an original idea. But the intellectual's input may well be instrumental in bringing about policy that is substantially different from what it would have been without that involvement.

Moreover, intellectuals have a major, though indirect, input into policy decisions by moulding the climate of ideas, and the general perspectives, or defining the situation in whose framework policy decisions are made. As C. H. Weiss (1977, p. 17) writes,

> social science research is used. It is not the kind of use most people have in mind when they hear the word. Not here the imminent decision, the single datum, the weighing of alternative options and shazam! Officials apparently use social science as a general guide to reinforce their sense of the world and make sense of that part of it that is still unmapped or confusing.

Thus, according to Weiss, the intellectuals' involvement in domestic policy has produced a common language of discourse including concepts such as achievement scores, self-esteem, upward mobility, social role, leadership structure, externalities, poverty, oppression, disorganization, deviance, mobilization, pressure groups and government responsiveness. Many of these concepts and notions imply a redefinition of problems and thereby offer a new perspective for considering solutions. According to R. E. Licklider (1971), the American intellectuals' involvement in foreign and military policy-related research has also produced a whole complex of related concepts and ideas such as those of deterrence, credible threats, first and second strike forces, counterforce and countervalue targeting, stable and unstable deterrents and arms control. 'Moreover', continues Licklider, 'this body of ideas had significant effects on the policy of the United States government' (ibid., p. 273).

Thus, although it may be difficult to pinpoint one concrete policy that was determined by intellectuals, they have helped create the conceptual framework and the framework of ideas in which both domestic and foreign/military policy were constructed and herein lies their major impact on policy.

Not only some general statements, but more systematic evidence on this type of influence by intellectuals on policy decisions has also accumulated. Thus Caplan *et al.* (1975), Knorr (1977), Patton *et al.* (1977) and Rich (1977), who all studied governmental agencies, found that decision-makers tended to use research results extensively, but mainly as general bases of information and as a source of conceptions to reorient their sense of the situation.

In sum, then, it would be true to say with Weiss (1977, p. 8) that the reports social science researchers now write 'need not find their final resting place in other researchers' footnotes but can make a difference in health care or education or economic policy'.

CONCLUSION

In this chapter various routes of influence by intellectuals on socio-political developments have been traced. Academics (scientists, social scientists, scholars in law and the humanities) all disseminate their ideas (via their teaching and writing) through their students, the future elites. In addition, natural and physical scientists further their ideas primarily through their impact on the technology of health, industry and warfare, while social scientists and scholarly experts in law further theirs mainly through their (direct or indirect) access to political parties and governmental structures. Here intellectuals can be seen to have a considerable share in constructing socio-political reality for policy-makers. Thereby they can also be seen to have an indirect but very significant effect on the shaping of policies. Through all these routes the socio-political influence of intellectuals can be seen to have increased in recent years. But whether the intellectuals' contribution in these respects is a worthwhile one and whether, therefore, their growing influence is a welcome development, is another matter which is dealt with in the next part of the book.

NOTES: CHAPTER 2

1   For instance, the influence of journalists through the media.

Part Two

THE ARGUMENT

3

The Intellectuals in Post-Industrial Society: an Alternative View

The growing influence of intellectuals in modern society (surveyed in the previous chapter) has not gone unnoticed. It has been emphasized for instance (and perhaps somewhat over-emphasized) by a group of scholars who have converged on the idea of the Knowledge Class in the 'post-industrial', 'technetronic' or similarly termed, society. These scholars have also asserted, however, that the growing influence of the Knowledge Class (which includes intellectuals)[1] has increasingly worked for the benefit of society – a claim I dispute. It is to this dispute that the present chapter is devoted.

THE CONCEPTION OF THE KNOWLEDGE CLASS IN POST-INDUSTRIAL SOCIETY

A conception which has become popular, though controversial, in recent years (propounded, for instance, by Bell, 1973; Boulding, 1964; Brzezinski, 1970; Galbraith, 1967; Drucker, 1971; Toffler, 1980; and others) holds that industrial-capitalist society is practically defunct and that a new type of society is now coming into being. In industrial society production was at the centre of socio-economic life. In contrast, the most distinctive feature of the new society lies in its crystallization around the organization and control of theoretical knowledge. This knowledge now forms the basis of technology and policies which have produced an era of abundance, equity and liberty.

Ideas such as these have been expressed, for instance, by Z. Brzezinski (1970) in the following words:

The post industrial society is becoming a 'technetronic' society. In the 'technetronic' society scientific and technical knowledge, in addition to enhancing production capabilities, quickly spills over to affect almost all aspects of life directly. (pp. 9–10)
In the technetronic society the university becomes an intensely involved 'think tank', the source of much sustained political planning and social innovation. (p. 12)
The positive potential of the Third American Revolution (i.e. the technetronic revolution) lies in its promise to link liberty with equality ... linked to political reform, the current cultural revolution could gradually enlarge the scope of personal freedom ... and give greater meaning to equality by making knowledge the basis of social and racial egalitarianism. (p. 273)

Ideas of this kind have been most forcefully expressed by D. Bell in his book *The Coming of the Post Industrial Society* (1973), in which he writes that the axial principle of post-industrial society is 'the centrality of theoretical knowledge as the source of innovation and of policy formulation for the society' (p. 14).

In the post industrial society ... the crucial decisions regarding the growth of the economy and its balance will come from government but they will be based on the government's sponsorship of research and development ... (p. 344)
The rise of the new elites based on skill derives from the simple fact that knowledge and planning – military planning, economic planning, social planning – have become the basic requisites for all organized action in a modern society. The members of this new technocratic elite, with their new techniques of decision-making (systems analysis, linear programming, and program budgeting), have now become essential to the formulation and analysis of decisions on which political judgments have to be made ... (p. 362)
Every society now lives by innovation and growth and it is theoretical knowledge that has become the matrix of innovation. With the growing sophistication of simulation

procedures through the use of computers ... we have the possibility, for the first time, of large-scale 'controlled experiments' in the social sciences. These, in turn, will allow us to plot alternative futures in different courses, thus greatly increasing the extent to which we can choose and control matters that affect our lives. (p. 344)

For the first time in human history ... the problem of survival in the bare sense of the word – freedom from hunger and disease – need no longer exist. The question before the human race is not subsistence but standard of living. Basic needs are satiable and the possibility of abundance is real. (p. 465)

A striking fact of Western society over the past two hundred years has been the steady decrease in the disparity among persons – not by distribution policies and judgment about fairness, but by technology which has cheapened the cost of products and made more things available to more people. (p. 451)

Somewhat similar ideas have been expressed by certain European thinkers, notably Raymond Aron (1967) and Alain Touraine (1971). These thinkers, too, see knowledge as having an increasing impact on society, as leading to greater rationality in production and hence to greater prosperity. But they do not claim that this necessarily results in social progress. Thus Aron writes that 'the quality of existence is not determined by the amount of goods available to each person' (1967, p. 80). And Touraine posits that post-industrial society has become a society of pervasive manipulation and alienation.

My argument, therefore, is primarily with the American post-industrialists from whose writings (as illustrated above) three major relevant themes emerge.

1 In technetronic or post-industrial society theoretical knowledge is increasingly suited for, and serving as the basis of, production and the formulation of policy.
2 The process of joining theoretical knowledge with production and policy formation – the distinct social contribution of the Knowledge Class – is increasingly

beneficial for Western society in that it has increasingly enabled it to plan and control its own destiny.
3 As a result, Western society has recently become more affluent and egalitarian, has afforded its citizens greater freedom, and is likely to do so to an even greater extent in the future.

AN ALTERNATIVE VIEW

The argument I would like to develop here is, almost on every count, the exact opposite. My claim is that:

1 The creation of theoretical knowledge (engaged in by intellectuals or the Knowledge Elite) and the formulation of policy (by politicians and bureaucrats) are two inherently disparate forms of human endeavour, and there is a formidable gap between the two, which can be bridged only with great difficulty.
2 The practical application of theoretical knowledge is, in general, exceedingly problematic. Its results may be beneficial for society but are not necessarily so.
3 In recent years, theoretical knowledge, though increasingly applied for practical usage, and though affording more social influence to its creators, has not become more beneficial for Western society. On the contrary, the benefits of theoretical knowledge, and the advice based on it, have recently petered out while the deleterious effects of that knowledge have become more prominent.
4 Western society is no longer becoming more affluent, egalitarian and free with the aid of that knowledge. On the contrary, it is facing mounting problems, to which the knowledge-based advice tendered by intellectuals has itself contributed.

While all this should now be common knowledge it is not usually stated in a straightforward manner by intellectuals, and frequently is even obscured by them. *This is so because in laying claim to the ever greater public funds on which the livelihood and social position of their own growing numbers depend, intellectuals have increasingly had to legitimize their endeavour – the creation of theoretical knowledge – through its presumed social benefits.* Indeed, the ideas expressed by the post-industrialists may well be seen as part of this process of legitimation.

The recent squeeze on funding for higher education and research has made it more important than ever for the Knowledge Elite to legitimize its endeavour by convincing the public of the usefulness of knowledge. *Hence the Knowledge Elite has become especially persuasive concerning the beneficial effect of knowledge for policies – precisely when it has become evident that these policies are not as effective as was previously thought.* This has come about largely after most post-industrialists have had their say, but it has contributed to making their claims about the role of the so-called Knowledge Class in post-industrial society questionable, if not obsolete.

One problem with the ideas converged upon by post-industrialists is that they lump together the theoretical knowledge furnished by social-behavioural sciences and the humanities on the one hand and that supplied by the natural and physical or exact sciences on the other. Their ideas seem to be based on the implicit assumption that the relationship between both types of knowledge and society is, if not identical, at least very similar. They are based on the assumption that both types of knowledge are of equal use to society. In contrast, I will make the case that they are not only very different types of knowledge but that their linkages with society are of a very different nature even though the final results of those linkages may be comparable.

Intellectuals of the social sciences and the humanities have purported to provide knowledge as the basis for *policies* which would guide society towards a better future. Intellectuals of the natural and physical sciences have purported to supply knowledge whose *practical application* would lead society towards a better future. Both have failed but for different reasons.

In the social sciences and the humanities the mishaps have come about because of a basic gulf between theoretical knowledge and practical policy guidelines. In the natural and physical sciences the gap is not so much between theory and practice as between practice and benefit. Here the problems have come about not so much because of a rift between knowledge and application as because of one between application and usefulness.

Many intellectuals of all types have (metaphorically speaking) presented themselves as prophets. But different types of intellectuals have done so in different ways. In this context Popper (1957) made the apt distinction between conditional or technological predictions ('if x then y') and prophecies ('y will occur'). The exact sciences, he wrote, typically make conditional predictions; the social sciences and humanities typically produce prophecies. This distinction still seems to be a useful one today. For since it was made, over a quarter of a century ago, a growing number of intellectuals in the social sciences and humanities have indeed purported to use theoretical knowledge as a basis for prophecies or forecasts into the future. More often than not this was to be a rosy future which knowledge (supplied by themselves) would help bring about. Intellectuals in the natural and physical sciences, typically limiting themselves to conditional predictions, have been less prone to use their theoretical knowledge as a basis for plunges into the future. But they have supplied the knowledge whose application would supposedly contribute towards a better future. It is now becoming evident that both types of endeavour have been equally dubious.

THE SITUATION IN THE SOCIAL SCIENCES AND THE HUMANITIES

The presumed relevance of the social sciences and the humanities for society lies first and foremost in the policy area.[2] *It is my argument, however, that the creation of theoretical knowledge in the humanities and social sciences and the formation of policy fundamentally diverge from each other; the criteria for their success are entirely different and their struggles for survival proceed along entirely dissimilar routes.*

Theoretical knowledge in the social sciences and the humanities is made up of sets of cognitive statements about social reality and the human condition. To prove its worth it must, in the first place, be innovative and original; it must, in the second place, be plausible and convincing; and it must, in the third place, be internally consistent. It is only by meeting these criteria that it stands the chance of attaining the status of a notable intellectual contribution.

A policy, on the other hand, is a series of guidelines for action. To become acceptable it must, in the first place, be geared to the fulfilment of widely accepted or powerfully supported goals (including the solution of vexing problems). It must, in the second place, put those goals in widely accepted or powerfully supported orders of priority. It must, in the third place, hold the promise of showing tangible results in meeting these goals. It must, in the fourth place, be economically feasible and cost-effective. Finally, it must be appealing to large sections of the relevant public and/or to powerful interest groups, and thus show the potential of gaining strong political support. It is only by meeting these criteria that it has a chance of being put into practice.

By the same token, the struggle for survival of an intellectual contribution and that of a policy proposal proceed along different paths. The former proceeds through argumentation within the intellectual community, the latter through appearance on the agenda of political and/or administrative decision-making bodies. The former thrives on criticism and controversy, the latter's chances of survival diminish through opposition. The former has won the battle for survival when it is frequently acknowledged in its original form; the latter can only win the battle for survival when passing through a series of compromises between different interests. Finally, the reward a successful intellectual contribution brings its originator is mainly recognition and attention, while the reward a successful policy formation brings to those in charge of it is primarily power.

In view of these basic disparities between theoretical knowledge in the social sciences and humanities on the one hand and policy on the other, it stands to reason that bridging the gap between them is exceedingly problematic. Yet this is precisely what intellectuals claim to have done, as they have increasingly legitimized their intellectual endeavour of creating knowledge by the extrinsic criteria of its applicability to policy formation for the greater benefit of society.

In a sense, this tendency of the Knowledge Elite to legitimize its endeavour by stressing its contribution to the welfare of society harks back to a longstanding tradition. Ever since the beginnings of modernity, and especially since the Enlightenment, reason, knowledge and particularly science came to be associated in Western thought with social progress. Advancing knowledge, and those who wielded it, were to lead to the conquest of nature and to a better understanding of society, and would thus lead humanity towards perfectibility and greater happiness.

Ideas such as these were subsequently perpetuated into the nineteenth century by thinkers like Henri de Saint-Simon and Auguste Comte whose dominant conviction was that intellectual progress would lead to social progress, and who emphasized the role of science (and social science) in controlling, guiding and advancing society. Later on the Fabians, the German academic socialists and the American liberals of the 1920s and 1930s all took for granted the powerful, beneficial effect of applying reason, knowledge and, in particular science, to the economy, to the creation of social policy and to the planning of society's future.

Nevertheless, as long as universities were small, their students few, and the public funds required to sustain them minimal, knowledge in the humanities and the social sciences could still find its legitimation mainly intrinsically – as knowledge for its own sake, without having to prove its practical utility for society. Concomitantly its creators had to legitimize themselves primarily inside rather than outside the intellectual establishment.

Subsequently, however, the role and size of universities changed. From centres for the creation of knowledge, and of small elites of experts in that knowledge, universities turned into centres for the training, selection and accreditation of larger and greater varieties of elites and for desired occupations in general. The growth in the numbers of students receiving their training and accreditation in universities went hand in hand with a growth in the numbers of intellectuals now in charge of their training and accreditation. Among the growing elites (of whose training and accreditation intellectuals were now in charge) was a growing number of potential intellectuals. These in turn made possible, and created pressures for, the further growth of universities and research institutes to absorb their own proliferating numbers.

Eventually, and especially since the Second World War, as institutions of higher learning and research reached formidable proportions, as they demanded and were granted increasing resources for their social sciences and humanities endeavours, intrinsic legitimation of knowledge no longer sufficed. Because of the enormous public funds now demanded for and invested in education and research in the social sciences and in some of the humanities (as described in Chapter 2), scholars in these disciplines now felt increasingly called upon to demonstrate that they provided society with more than bits of esoteric knowledge of interest to no one but themselves. As P. H. Rossi in his presidential address to the 1980 American Sociological Association stated: 'And when it comes to facing outward toward the public – and especially toward our benefactors – we are very quick to point to the many complicated social problems that justify our existence and need for support' (Rossi, 1980, p. 889). Or as A. Cherns (1979, pp. 3–4) explains: 'Whether explicit or not, claims made by social scientists for resources carry implications about the potential use to which social science is to be put.'

For their part, governments and related bodies have also put increasing emphasis on the potential benefits of the social sciences for the state and society. In recent years these presumed benefits have been brought out by various official reports, such as the US House of Representatives Report (1967), the National Academy of Sciences Report (1968) and the National Science Foundation Report (1969) in the United States, or the British Academy Report (1961) and the Heyworth Committee Report (1965) in Britain. And the 'emphasis on the potential use of social science research has grown with each of these succeeding publications' (Cherns, 1979, p. 5). Thus a dual process has taken place, whereby members of the Knowledge Elite have increasingly claimed legitimacy (and funds) for their endeavour by presenting it as beneficial for society, while governments have increasingly justified their growing expenditures in these areas by the same criteria.

The increasing availability of funds has itself led to an increase in the type of activities that could be justified as beneficial for society and, in particular, to an increase in policy-related, that is, applied research. Rossi (1980, p. 901) aptly summarized the situation for the United States:

Within the last decade new organizations have appeared on the scene to provide the applied social research that was demanded by the existence of research funds. Older, non academic research organizations have also responded by increasing their staff.

This in turn, has led to a further need to find justification or legitimation for applied research.

In recent years – with the growing economic difficulties in many Western countries, with the financial squeeze on universities and research institutes, with the tightening employment prospects for students and academics – the necessity of providing a broader legitimation for the activities of intellectuals in the humanities and social sciences has been felt even more urgently. In their scramble for shrinking resources these intellectuals have thus increasingly been led to present their disciplines as 'relevant' in terms of preparing their students for viable careers and in terms of the usefulness of their research for policy formation. And policy-makers seem to have (perhaps reluctantly) continued to accept this presentation of self on the part of the social sciences. In Anderson and Biddle's (1982) words: 'The straitened financial circumstances in which many social research agencies find themselves is causing individuals on both sides of the research policy fence to make loud assertions concerning the value of research.'

These assertions are best illustrated by a recent survey of 100 social researchers in Australia by D. Anderson (1983) who found that practically all respondents saw their studies as pertinent for policy, practically all believed that policy ought to be influenced by social science research evidence and practically all believed that it ought to be influenced by such evidence to a greater extent than is actually the case at present. They are also well illustrated by the summary claim recently made on behalf of the social sciences by one of their most prominent representatives, A. H. Halsey (1983, p. 4), as follows: 'If we wish to deliver a more intelligent and responsible democracy to our children than we have ourselves contrived to practice, we will either use social science or act against our collective interest.' Thus the increase of available public resources especially since the Second World War, and (paradoxically) the tightening of such resources during the last few years, have both led to increasing emphasis being put on the extrinsic legitimation of the intellectual endeavour.

To present their endeavour as socially useful some social scientists have presented a rather simplistic model on the use of research for policy formation. Weiss (1977, pp. 11–12) describes this as a linear model whereby 'a problem exists; information or understanding is lacking . . . research provides the missing knowledge; a solution is reached'. Needless to say, this is not only an oversimplification but, indeed, a mis-representation of actual reality. For by its very nature, the knowledge produced by social science research is always piecemeal, incomplete and tentative. Because of the complexity of social issues, not all relevant aspects of a problem can usually be taken into account in even a multivariate research design. In focusing on some aspects, research frequently leaves out others whose inclusion might have led to different results. Research projects conducted on different populations often come up with contradictory or inconsistent empirical evidence; the evidence itself is almost invariably open to contrasting interpretations which almost invariably lead to different implications for action. As R. Mayntz (1977) notes, social scientists are well aware of the tentative nature of their knowledge. Yet in tendering policy advice they are apt to forget this fact and accept speculative ideas as a valid, proven account of social reality. The knowledge emanating from social science research thus rarely supplies straightforward answers to policy-related questions, but social scientists are frequently tempted to present it as such.

As has become widely recognized, some intellectuals of the social sciences and humanities have gone even further than that. To present themselves as socially useful, they have increasingly borrowed the halo from, and basked in the glory of, the natural and physical sciences. They have increasingly presented their knowledge as consisting of empirically testable (and sometimes even tested) scientific theories, and hence as ready to be utilized for practical purposes.

In fact, however, most of the intellectual output provided by the social sciences and humanities does not provide a set of definitive statements on the relationships among variables from which empirically testable hypotheses can be derived. Rather, the sets of cognitive systems scholars in the social sciences and humanities create are mostly what Merton (1957, p. 87) referred to as general orientations towards human or social reality. While this term was coined some three decades ago, it seems that in this area little has changed since then. Much of what the humanities and social sciences provide is still in the nature of conceptual frameworks and general approaches to the human condition, in the nature of *Weltanschauungen*, more than anything else. They provide spectacles that enhance our sight and sensitize us to various aspects of human life. Through them we may view humanity and social life with more insight and more systematically than would be possible with common sense alone. But by their very nature these theories are not empirically testable in any conclusive manner.[3]

To be sure, much empirical research has in fact been carried out to follow up these theories and much (and perhaps more than ever before) is still being carried out today. But none of it has ever led to the conclusive refutation of any such theory, be it 'mainstream' or Marxist, be it Keynesian or Friedmanite, or any other sort. And while empirical research has led to the recognition of limited uniformities it has rarely if ever led to the establishment of 'laws' on which we can depend with any degree of confidence.

The explanation for this has to do not (as some have claimed) with the relative youth of the behavioural sciences but (as others have claimed) with the complexities and idiosyncrasies of human nature and with problems of free volition, and are beyond the scope of this discussion. What is of relevance, however, is that because the intellectuals in the social sciences and humanities provide mostly *Weltanschaungen* rather than testable theories, the policy advice emanating from them is really based on their originators' value judgements more than on their knowledge of facts, causes and consequences. It is based on ideas about what ought to be more than on rigorous knowledge of what actually is or of what will happen when a certain policy is put into practice. It shows, in I. L. Horowitz's (1971, p. 8) words, 'how little we know about how things ought to work'.

However, the value judgements of social scientists, of experts in the humanities, or indeed of any other intellectuals, though they sometimes assume the mantle of scientific knowledge, in fact have no greater validity than anybody else's value judgements. Hence there is little reason to believe that policy decisions in one way or another influenced by the advice of social scientists have been morally superior to what they otherwise would have been.

Further, because no theory in the humanities and social sciences has ever been conclusively refuted, many mutually contradictory theories co-exist peacefully (or not so peacefully) in the same disciplines, frequently gathering disciples who are in constant disputation with one another. Within the intellectual community such disputations are entirely proper and appropriate. Indeed, the various disciplines in the humanities and social sciences thrive on such controversies and the persons promoting them thrive on them intellectually as well as career-wise. But in the policy area such controversy is the source of much confusion. As policy-makers attempt to find their way in the maze of the various approaches, as they also attempt to effect the various inevitable compromises without which policy proposals can rarely come to fruition, they are not infrequently disowned by the originators of these approaches. Policy-makers are thus frequently at a loss to know whether those approaches themselves, or their own lack of aptitude, or else the attempted compromises are to be blamed for policy failures.

Moreover, as Mayntz (1977) has, once more, correctly perceived, the recent increase in research activity has tended to multiply approaches. This, in turn, has generally added to rather than detracted from the mystification of policy-making. The more social science research has prospered, the harder has it been to obtain clear policy guidelines on its basis.

As a consequence of all this, there is no reason to believe that more social science research and knowledge in recent years has led to improved policy decisions, to more effective actions, and hence to the reduction of social problems. On the contrary, although no causality can be shown, it is nevertheless worth noting that the years in which the influence of the social scientists on policy has been growing have also been the years in which policy failures have been rife and in which a variety of formidable social problems have been multiplying. This will be shown in greater detail in the next chapter and illustrated again in Chapter 5.

THE SITUATION IN THE NATURAL AND PHYSICAL SCIENCES

In the natural and physical sciences the problems are of a different nature, yet with comparable results. The practical utilization of these sciences usually takes place not directly through policy formation but through the medium of technology, for instance, for the development of medicine, industrial production, or armaments.[4] Hence the fact that the creation of theoretical knowledge in these areas and the formation of policy are inherently disparate forms of human endeavour is not so relevant here. Further, although the natural and the physical sciences have also had to justify their endeavour to the outside world through the practical results of their knowledge, they have found it easier to cope with this problem of legitimacy, because those practical results have been so much more clearly visible.

I claim, however, that despite all this there still is a gulf between theoretical knowledge in the physical and natural sciences on the one hand and the practical benefits of that knowledge for society on the other hand. *This gulf derives from the fact that although in the exact sciences knowledge is frequently usable it is not necessarily useful for society*; as is now increasingly recognized, its practical results may be beneficial as well as harmful.

Bell (1973) has argued that although science-based technological advances may have deleterious effects on society these can be eliminated through alternative social arrangements. In contrast, I argue that such deleterious effects, no less than the beneficial ones, are inherent in the very nature of scientific knowledge and its practical results, *as well as* in certain social arrangements which exacerbate the problem. Therefore, I argue, the adverse effects of scientific knowledge (no less than the beneficial ones) *are actually built into the socio-political role of the scientist.* The post-industrialists have argued that the beneficial effects of scientific knowledge have become more prominent in recent years. In contrast, I argue that it is precisely in recent years that the practical results of the knowledge provided by the natural and physical sciences, and hence the role of the scientist, have become exceedingly problematic.

Since its inception, science has been both greatly revered and fiercely attacked. But the attacks on science come in different varieties (see Passmore, 1978). My own version is that the detrimental effects of science (no less than its beneficial effects) are inherent in the nature and practical results of science because these results are cumulative as well as value-neutral. The cumulative nature of the practical results of science – the very feature that leads to more and more discoveries and inventions – also makes it practically inevitable that (if only by chance) some of these discoveries and inventions will have harmful potential. The value-neutral nature of science implies that there is nothing to prevent harmful (as well as beneficial) discoveries from being made. The combination of the two factors practically ensures that this will actually happen.

Let us take each of these factors in turn. Are the practical results of physical and natural science indeed cumulative? The answer to this question is ostensibly self-evident. Yet problems arise because two diametrically opposed views on the essence of science are prevalent today. According to the first approach, primarily associated with Karl Popper, scientific knowledge consists of theories subject to falsification through rigorous procedures of empirical testing. Science progresses because new theories provide a closer fit with empirical reality than theories which are consequently discarded. According to the second view, of which Thomas Kuhn is the forerunner, the procedures and conclusions of science are the contingent outcome of interpretive social processes. Scientific theories, even in the natural and physical sciences, can never be conclusively tested (and refuted) by empirical evidence. Hence the history of science has not been a smooth process of growth whereby old and less valid theories have been replaced by new and more valid ones. Rather this history is wrought with periodical upheavals which lead to discontinuities and redirections of the scientific effort (see Weingart, 1974; Feyerabend, 1975; Mulkay, 1979a and 1979b; Laudan, 1981; and others).

In recent years the first approach has been losing ground in the scholarly community while the second approach has been gaining ground. According to some more moderate representatives of the second approach, however, growth of scientific knowledge is not entirely precluded. Thus Laudan, for instance, is hardly a Popperian. Yet in some of Laudan's writings (1977, 1979) the claim that science grows is defended. And Mulkay, one of the representatives of the second approach, explicitly states that science involves a 'cumulative increase in the rate of knowledge production' (1979a, p. 72).

Furthermore, adherents of the first school of thought have by no means accepted defeat and recently have attempted a comeback with an amended view. In other words, some scholars now claim that 'scientific discovery is being rediscovered' (Nickels, 1980, p. v). With these scholars I would argue that discontinuities and redirections do not preclude scientific growth; that it would be implausible to maintain that since its inception Western science has not grown at all. In fact there has been a certain evolution or growth of scientific knowledge[5] through a process of critical selection. By this process outmoded scientific theories have been replaced by new ones that are 'fitter for survival'. This fitness in turn hinges on a number of overlapping criteria including better explanatory power over more aspects of empirical reality, more testable hypotheses that have not been refuted, more consequences whose applications help one control nature, greater ability to solve existent problems, and greater potential of generating new problems for subsequent solution (see Lakatos, 1972; Popper, 1972; Toulmin, 1972; Gibson, 1973; Shapere, 1974; Putnam, 1975; Hardin and Rosenberg, 1982; see also Böhme, 1977). In the natural and physical sciences, then, the replacement of outmoded theories by newer ones has actually led to a process of development and growth of scientific knowledge.

If scientific knowledge can be said to be growing, then its practical results must necessarily be cumulative. This is so, at least in a very simplistic sense, in that new knowledge gives rise to new discoveries. These serve as starting points for more discoveries and for inventions – which serve as bases for further inventions.

Recently the claim has been made that the link between science and technology is not as straightforward as has previously been thought. It has been claimed that even in the natural and physical sciences the relationship between theoretical knowledge and practical application is frequently tenuous, that practical discoveries are sometimes developed by trial and error rather than on the basis of theory, and that sometimes the development of science is a spin-off from the development of technology rather than the other way around (see Gibbons and Johnson, 1970; McKeown, 1976; Layton, 1977; Mulkay, 1977 and 1979a; and others). This is not to say, however, that the relationship between science and technology is nonexistent. Even according to the authors who make the above-mentioned claims, many practical developments can be traced back to scientific knowledge. This is so, although often this may be elementary or older scientific knowledge and although sometimes practical applications can be traced back to their scientific antecedents only in a roundabout way. According to several of the same observers, moreover, the relationship between science and technology, between theoretical knowledge and practical results, has become more prominent in recent years.

Hence my argument, as stated above, that in the natural and physical sciences (in contrast to the social sciences and the humanities) the most significant gap is not between theoretical knowledge and practical results, but between the practical results of knowledge and its benefits. Practical effects of science are not necessarily good effects; some of these effects are clearly detrimental to society. Therefore, as effects accumulate and multiply, the chances of detrimental effects coming about (side by side with beneficial ones) multiply as well.

This is so also because the practical results of science (no less than science itself) are value-neutral. To be sure, values influence the institutional arrangements surrounding science and the actions of scientists. This knowledge, in turn, has implications for values (see Martin, 1979). But in the natural and physical sciences (as distinct from the social sciences and humanities) the scientific statement as such is value-free. And so are the practical implications of that statement. That is to say, there is nothing in the inner logic or in the inherent structure of science to prevent lowly valued (as well as highly valued), detrimental (as well as beneficial) discoveries from being made. Hence the more discoveries accumulate, the greater the probability that some of them will have unpalatable or even destructive effects on society.

Of course, these destructive effects do not necessarily have to be put into practice. But scientific knowledge, once learned, cannot be unlearned. Discoveries, once made, cannot be undiscovered. Unlike the legendary genie, undesirable scientific knowledge, once unleashed, cannot be forced back into a corked bottle. It is always there and readily available.

The destructive potential inherent in science itself is further exacerbated by certain social arrangements and developments which have become more prominent in recent years and are largely irreversible. For instance, the social structure of science is such that knowledge created by scientists cannot be validated except through the judgement and verdict of other scientists. The dissemination of scientific knowledge within the scientific community is thus part and parcel of the institutional arrangements surrounding science, and part of the role of the scientists in society. Hence detrimental (no less than beneficial) scientific knowledge is being constantly disseminated. And the larger the international scientific community grows, the more widely is detrimental knowledge diffused, and the larger the number of people in command of that knowledge. Hence the confidence that we may have in the effects of that knowledge not being realized becomes weaker. At the same time the threats to the very existence of humanity emanating from that knowledge loom larger.

Another social pattern which exacerbates the harmful effects of science is the increasing pressure being put on scientists to produce practical results. This is not a new development, of course. The general (previously mentioned) expectation that the intellectual endeavour and the knowledge it produces would be of service to humanity, which became prevalent in Western society especially from the seventeenth century onwards, was aimed first and foremost at the natural and physical sciences. But as Merton (1973, pp. 185–6) writes, once science had established itself, it was widely accepted as a value in its own right, and only as a 'surplus value' was it expected to lead to practical consequences.

In recent years, however, the pressures for practical results of scientific research have clearly mounted. Throughout the twentieth century more physical and natural scientists have been needed (and have emerged) to train the growing numbers of those who wish to join the community of scientists (see Mulkay, 1977, p. 123). This in turn has led to the need for more funding for increasing numbers of teaching and research positions. Lately the numbers of scientists have not been growing as before, but by now their numbers have become large enough to staff a wide variety of newly created positions, including a large number of positions in applied research.

At the same time, there has been increasing demand and increasing support for scientific research from both the government and the private sector. With the development of scientific research technology, support for that research has greatly increased in cost. This has led both government and private enterprise to require more tangible returns for their investment; which is but another way of saying that more and more scientists have now come to occupy positions in which they are under constant pressure to produce practical results. Thus this pressure is now institutionalized into their social roles and positions. And, to reiterate, the more such practical results accumulate, the greater the chances that they will include destructive (besides productive) elements.

As the advances in science and their practical utilization are not evenly distributed over time, there may be certain periods in history when their benefits have (temporarily perhaps) been exhausted or diminished while their deleterious implications become more formidable. It seems that we have now reached such a time in history. Support for this thesis with respect to natural and physical scientists' contribution to medicine, weaponry and production is presented in Chapter 6.

CONCLUSION

In sum, then, the argument presented in this chapter runs counter to that of the post-industrialists. It holds that the application of theoretical knowledge produced by intellectuals in the social sciences and the humanities on the one hand, and in the natural and physical sciences on the other, entails some major problems. The argument also holds that although these problems are of a different nature, their implications are similar. Because of them, the beneficial effects of theoretical knowledge for society cannot be taken for granted. It holds that both in the social sciences and the humanities and in the natural and physical sciences these problems have become (albeit for different reasons) more noticeable in recent years.

Recently, intellectuals in the social sciences and the humanities and in the natural and physical sciences have both promised good things for society but (for different reasons) have not really produced them. In some (though different) ways they have both created problems for society. Yet both have been under mounting pressure to legitimize their role in society by the supposed benefits neither of them could really deliver. This argument is further developed in the next chapter.

NOTES: CHAPTER 3

1 See Chapter 1.
2 This may, of course, include production policy and it refers to the policy of a government, an enterprise, or any other social unit.

3 The question of the extent to which theories in the natural and physical sciences are so testable is dealt with briefly below.
4 At the same time the technological advances provided, as well as science itself, can of course serve as objects of policy.
5 Although different disciplines in the natural and physical sciences have, of course, differed in the extent of their growth.

4

The Intellectuals in a Groping Society

One point that remains to be discussed with regard to the post-industrialists concerns their conceptions of the Knowledge Class's (including intellectuals') provision of knowledge, as increasingly helping post-industrial society take hold of its own fate and move towards greater prosperity, equality and freedom. Such conceptions (examples of which have been presented at the beginning of the previous chapter) made good sense at the beginning of the 1970s when they were published. They also seemed to provide, at the same time, a convincing forecast of the direction in which things were heading. Now, a decade later, however, they no longer present an acceptable image of the so-called Knowledge Class and the society that supposedly benefits from its knowledge.

The image of Western society that emerges today is more that of a groping society which is increasingly overwhelmed by the complexity of its own problems and its ever more pronounced internal contradictions. And the Knowledge Class, and intellectuals in particular, may best be seen as groping together with the rest of society in the face of those increasingly intractable problems.

Some of the problems and contradictions with which Western society is now groping are well known; others are just coming to the fore. In any case it is worth mentioning some major ones briefly *not for their own sake but for the purpose of showing the intellectuals' brilliance in analysing them as contrasted with their inefficacy in dealing with them in practice.*

THE PROBLEM OF GOVERNMENTAL OVERLOAD

One of these problems is what a number of intellectual scholars have identified as 'governmental overload'. As these scholars (including Bell himself) have convincingly suggested, the growing complexity of modern society and the expanding role of governments in the economy and society have recently led to a vastly greater complexity of government tasks. Also, there has recently been a growth of pressures on government to meet an array of vastly expanding demands. These demands result from a revolution of entitlements: an increasing expectation on the part of an increasing number of groups that the government is responsible for fulfilling their needs, and an escalation in what these groups conceive their needs to be (Huntington, 1968; Bell, 1975; Crozier *et al.*, 1975; King, 1975; Rose, 1979). Just about all grievances now get dumped into the lap of government. Government has come to be regarded as 'a sort of unlimited liability insurance company, in the business of ensuring all persons at all times against every conceivable risk' (King, 1975, p. 286). 'Once upon a time, then, man looked to God to order the world. Then he looked to the market. Now he looks to government' (p. 288).

Governments, however (and those who advise them), have trouble trying to play God. For the increasing demands on, and responsibilities of, governments have not been matched by governments' increasing capacity to meet those demands and shoulder those responsibilities. This is evidenced by the fact that many government policies do not fulfil the expectations pinned on them, do not lead to any visible improvements in whatever they were meant to improve and (in Schultze's 1977, p. 2, somewhat extreme formulation) consist principally of 'throwing money at problems'.

Thus, today, the acceptable image is no longer that of knowledge-based, well-designed policies leading to widespread prosperity, but rather that of knowledge-based but confused policies leading to widespread frustration. As A. Wildavsky (1973, p. 27) puts it: 'The essential perversity of the policy milieu is its ability to frustrate nearly everyone at the same time.'

THE CRISIS OF THE WELFARE STATE

One apt illustration of this is that welfare state policies (as they have developed over the last century or so and as they have crystallized especially in the postwar era) have no longer been capable of coping with mounting needs and demands. As G. L. Field and J. Higley (1982, p. 13) see it:

> From the early postwar years down to the end of the 1970s the rationale of domestic policy in all western countries was that a combination of welfare state social insurance programmes and labour gains through collective bargaining would mitigate serious discontent and keep western social orders functioning effectively. Economic growth would create tax revenues needed to expand the welfare state, full employment would keep social insurance outlays to affordable levels, and there would be sufficient funds left over to provide an adequate defence against rival communist countries . . . In retrospect it is clear that this policy rationale was fatally undermined by economic and social developments during the 1970s.

The problems created for the welfare state by the economic setbacks of the 1970s were exacerbated by a related trend of growth in the public's expectations for government-provided welfare, coupled with a growth in the proportion of the Western population that is in need and/or entitled to special government (or government-supported) services and payments. Thus, for instance, there has been in recent years, all over the Western world an increase in the proportion of aged persons (and a diminishing readiness of families to care for them on their own).[1] Because of recently growing divorce and separation rates there is also an increase in the proportion of single-parent families,[2] another category of people at least potentially in need of government support. Further, there is in recent years, all over the Western world, an increase in the proportion of unemployed – yet another category of people in need of government assistance.

The recent rise in unemployment has been caused, in part, by the economic downturn of the 1970s. But a significant proportion of unemployment is widely considered to be 'structural', that is, based on long-term trends of technological change and increasing automation. Hence, even though economic recovery now seems to be on its way, and even though in some countries there has recently been a drop in unemployment,[3] there is no reason to hope that unemployment is instigating a major retreat and reverting to the erstwhile low levels of the postwar era. Also, in addition to the millions of people who are still registered as unemployed, millions of others are reported to be too discouraged to look for jobs. Many of them too, however, are (or will soon be) dependent on government welfare.

The fact that there has been a growth not only in the proportion of people in need of, but also in the proportion of people actually obtaining, government services is illustrated by the following figures. In the United States in 1950, 2·3 per cent of the population were social security beneficiaries; in 1960, 8·2 per cent of the population, and in 1981, 15·6 per cent of the population were social security beneficiaries. And this, of course, does not include additional types of welfare recipients whose total number is not so easily accessible. By some estimates, the number of all types of American welfare recipients totalled 8·9 million in 1950 and 60·6 million in 1982.[4] All this exerts practically irresistible pressures for growth in welfare expenditures and services and in the bureaucratic agencies rendering such services, another growing source of expenditure.

Not surprisingly, therefore, government expenditures on social services have actually been rising dramatically in recent years, even in countries in which New Right influenced regimes have done their best to curb such growth.[5] The general information reported in the press usually points to cuts in a variety of social services under the Reagan administration. Yet the expenditures on social services have clearly been rising. This seeming contradiction is explicable by the fact that (as reported before) the number of welfare recipients has been growing so dramatically that even when programmes are cut, expenses continue to grow. There is thus a practically irreversible trend for growth in welfare and social services related government expenditures.

Moreover, the growth in these expenditures has clearly exceeded economic growth. This is evident, for instance, from a recent study by the Organization for Economic Development (OECD) which shows that from 1960 to 1981 the cost of social programmes in its member countries grew nearly twice as fast as the economies of those countries.[6] A growing imbalance has thus been developing between government commitments and government resources. And yet the demands of the welfare state and government commitments to it keep increasing. This, combined with the increasing reluctance of the public to finance these commitments through ever-growing taxation, has led to what O'Connor (1973) has termed the fiscal crisis of the capitalist state.

Like social expenditures, the taxes which have made these expenditures possible have also grown in excess of economic development. Such taxes took up less than 10 per cent of Gross National Product around the turn of the century, and now comprise between a third and half of GNP in most Western countries.[7] Many income-earners have thus reached, if not the limits of their ability to pay, at least the limits of their willingness to do so. To be sure, there are still plenty of high profits that could be taxed more than they are now, and the taxation system could thus be rendered more equitable. But the fact that this has not been achieved is itself part of the fiscal crisis of the capitalist state, or of the capitalist welfare state. This is another problem which both non-Marxist and Marxist scholars have brilliantly analysed but from which knowledge-based policies (and those who provide the knowledge) have not been able to help extricate Western governments.

INEQUALITIES ARE NO LONGER DECREASING

In recent years the image invoked by post-industrialists of increasing prosperity and decreasing disparity has also become questionable. From the middle of the nineteenth century onwards and up until the postwar era, developments were in fact very much in line with that image. Both increasing prosperity and decreasing inequality have been amply documented. In nineteenth-century Europe working-class people lived under subhuman conditions while the rich accumulated more wealth. Towards the end of the nineteenth century, however, a substantial transformation was under way. Workers' real wages rose substantially though gradually; from 1860 to 1890 they rose by about 50–60 per cent in both Britain and America, and further substantial increases followed in subsequent years. In both Europe and America the long-term rise in real wages facilitated and was supplemented by improvements in the living environment, in health facilities and in rising consumption (Bagwell and Mingay, 1970).

As for inequality, Chirot (1977, p. 189) cites data showing that in the United States the top 5 per cent of income-earners received 30 per cent of the national income in 1929 but only 15·6 per cent in 1970. Similar data for other Western countries have been cited by Lydall (1968, ch. 6) and Broom and Jones (1976, p. 52).

Indeed, it has convincingly and often been argued that the relative stability of Western societies has been based to a large extent on growing affluence and on the fact that even those on the lower rungs of the socio-economic ladder have increasingly benefited from this affluence. A British Conservative leader, Stanley Baldwin, is reported to have said, 'If you want people to be conservative then given them something to conserve'. It seems that until recently Western societies have been able to do just that, by giving those lowest on the scale the sense that they are not much worse off than anyone else and that their situation is improving. Hence they have felt that they, too, have a stake in the system, and that (contrary to what Marx has claimed) by overthrowing it they have much more to lose than merely their chains. But recently the trends no longer point in the same direction.

There are some clear signs that for some time now inequalities have been decreasing only marginally, if at all. This is evident for the United States where the income share of the top 5 per cent of income-earners was reduced by almost 13 per cent from 1929 to 1950, but by merely less than 2 per cent between 1950 and 1970 (Chirot, 1977, p. 189). The same holds for Australia; Broom and Jones (1976, p. 52) report that from 1950 onwards the overall discrepancies amongst Australian income-earners remained more or less as they were. And a similar situation for other Western countries is reported and well analysed by Lydall (1968), Berthoud (1976) and Shanon (1975).[8]

What is noteworthy in particular is that inequalities stopped decreasing and stabilized at a point at which they were still very substantial. For instance, in the United States in 1970 the top fifth of income-earners enjoyed an income that was more than seven times as great as that obtained by the bottom fifth, and income inequalities in other Western countries equalled or exceeded those of the United States (see Ahluwalia, 1974, p. 8).

Wealth, moreover, is even more concentrated at the top. In most Western countries a small minority (the top 2–3 per cent of the population) own a considerable proportion (at least one-fifth) of all wealth, and hence wield a decisive share of economic power. Even worse, in some Western countries inequalities have recently been increasing. In both Australia and America, for instance, the gap between the top and the bottom income-earners has increased significantly since the 1960s and 1970s.[9]

UNEMPLOYMENT AND THE EMERGENCE OF AN 'UNDERCLASS'

What is particularly disturbing is that in the last decade, with the downturn of the Western economies and growing unemployment,[10] a distinctive phenomenon is becoming more visible: at the bottom of the class pyramid there is now crystallizing what G. Myrdal (1969) has aptly termed an 'underclass' of the long-term unemployed and unemployable. This small but significant category of people has been kept from starving by 'grudging and disreputable dole payments' (Field and Higley, 1982, p. 13). But besides suffering the indignity of failure, it has been forced to subsist on the threshold of poverty[11] or below. For instance, in the United States the number of persons living below the poverty line declined from 39·5 million in 1959 to 24·1 million in 1969, but since then has risen again to 29·3 million in 1980.[12]

This datum is of special significance, since intellectuals have offered several compelling explanations of poverty.[13] Intellectuals have also been involved in devising policies designed to eradicate poverty. For instance, American intellectuals connected with the Kennedy and Johnson administrations were heavily involved in the war against poverty in the 1960s. But as Daniel Moynihan in his book *Maximum Feasible Misunderstanding* (1969) and several other analysts (e.g. Preston, 1984) have shown, the success of the policies they devised was rather meagre. They generated much conflict among politicians and bureaucrats, thus turning the war *against* poverty into a war *over* poverty. But despite the fanfare they caused, little was achieved in the redistribution of resources. Poverty declined in the 1960s. But since the administrative measures inspired by intellectuals have been shown by practically all pertinent analyses to have been innocuous, it must be concluded that the decline in poverty was the result of the general economic growth taking place at the time and not the result of these measures. And indeed, the above figures show that as soon as economic conditions tightened poverty began rising again (see also Etzioni-Halevy, 1983a, ch. 13). And the conditions in several other countries are not much different.

All this means that a class structure has crystallized in which there is a certain proportion of the population that is not sharing in society's affluence. It is thus gaining only marginal benefits from the system, hence has only a marginal stake in it. It also means that a division has developed between the 'underclass' – whose benefits from the system are minimal, and all others (including the working class) – whose benefits from the system are substantial, though unequal. There are some signs that the 'underclass' now carries some of the destabilizing potential which Marx and Marxists have traditionally (and so far, wrongly) attributed to the working class, and which many social scientists thought no longer exists in Western society.

Thus far, such a destabilizing potential of the underclass has not manifested itself on a large scale. But it is quite possible that, being reduced to anomic circumstances, this group of people will revert to disruption through sporadic, often self-destructive, violent action (as they have done already in some instances). Such disruptive action, if it were to occur more frequently and on a larger scale than previously, could not but spell some unpleasant upheavals for Western capitalist societies.

Alternatively, this group of people may become increasingly distrustful of and alienated from society, as well as increasingly apathetic and passive politically. Once again, there are some preliminary signs that this is already occurring. An Australian Electoral Office Research Report (1983a and 1983b), for instance, indicates that most of the 600,000 Australians who are not enrolled for voting are young and many are unemployed. To establish the reasons for non-enrolment a series of discussions with groups of non-enrolled youngsters was held. In these discussions the unemployed stood out as alienated from the political system, as distrustful of its ability to meet their needs, as harbouring feelings of being rejected outsiders, and as having a sense of complete futility in bothering to vote at all. 'The unemployed stand out from all other groups in their attitudes because of the enormous feeling of rejection and the complete demoralization of their self esteem', the report says. 'Without exception, they feel that society, the system, has rejected them ... (p. 13). Such widespread feelings of distrust and alienation are almost as dangerous for Western society as sporadic violence, for they have the effect of de-legitimizing the system, thus paving the way for more noticeably destabilizing action later on.

In their capacity as scholars, intellectuals have offered numerous theories that include explanations not only for poverty but for unemployment as well. In their capacity as policy consultants intellectuals have tendered plentiful advice for alleviating it. But neither they nor those who base policies on their theories and advice have so far come up with tangible results. Since the Knowledge Elite has in fact been influential in shaping socio-economic policies and since it has taken part of the credit when these policies have been crowned with success, it seems only fair that it – that is to say, we – should accept part of the blame when successes are few and far between.

ALL IS NOT WELL WITH DEMOCRACY

Democracy is undoubtedly the most effective known political framework for the limitation of arbitrary elite power and for the enhancement and preservation of human rights and liberties, as a brief glance towards societies which lack this framework will readily show. It is also the most effective known framework for popular struggles to decrease inequalities. Indeed, the decreasing inequalities in Western societies from the nineteenth century onwards (documented above) can be traced back in large part to the institutionalization of the struggle over the distribution of resources in the then evolving democratic process. As such, democracy is one of Western society's most distinctive features, as well as one of its greatest assets.

But all is not well with Western democracy. Political freedoms are protected more than in other societies and inequalities are generally smaller.[14] But the fact that socio-economic gaps have no longer been decreasing in recent years, that they have stabilized at a point at which inequalities are still very great, that they have even been increasing again most recently, and that an underclass has been crystallizing at the bottom of the social hierarchy, is one of the indications of the present weaknesses of democracy. Related to this is a series of internal contradictions forming a potential threat for democracy, which have recently become more prominent and worrisome.

The question has recently been raised of how the formidable and growing power of the leadership of large-scale interest groups, and in particular that of business and industrial corporations on the one hand and labour unions on the other, as well as the growing power of bureaucracy, squares with the electoral principles of democracy. The plain answer, of course, is that it does not.

It would not be revealing much new to say that interest groups do not usually represent the general public. Moreover, not all interest groups have been equally capable of representing their own interests. As McConnell (1966) has correctly pointed out, 'some groups have used their opportunity with much greater effectiveness than others, for some, indeed, have been unable to seize the opportunity at all' (p. 26). The state's response to pressures, too, has been anything but egalitarian. Those who lack economic, social and political power, the poor, the minorities, in short the underprivileged, are most likely to have their pressures disregarded. The more articulate, the better established, the more powerful, are more likely to have their pressures responded to. There is thus something approaching a hierarchy of interest groups, with its top leadership in close symbiotic relations with the state's power-holding elites.

As observers of 'corporatism' have persuasively clarified, in many Western countries economic policy is increasingly worked out in close consultation between the state elites and the leadership of the most powerful interest groups: corporate organizations and labour unions (see e.g. Schmitter and Lehmbruch, eds, 1979). Neither, of course, are elected by the general public, and their increasing share in determining the country's fate renders that public's electoral power more and more innocuous.

Indeed, it is quite likely that the recently stabilized and growing inequalities and the coming to the fore of an underclass may be traced back, in large part, to these corporatist processes. Corporate organizations represent the interests of the privileged classes while trade unions represent, at least to some extent, their working-class members. But both represent relatively well established sectors of society, and because of their increasing political clout the interests of the less organized workers, of the unemployed, of the underclass, have no adequate representation in the political process. Hence they have no adequate representation in the political struggle over the distribution of resources.

Some internal contradictions for democracy have also been created by the role of bureaucracy in it. As many observers now agree, the top of the bureaucracy is also becoming increasingly powerful and independent from its formal superiors – the politicians. Since this is an appointed rather than an elected elite, atop an organization whose very principles contradict those of democracy, its growing power and independence clearly poses a threat to democracy. And yet a powerful, politically independent bureaucracy is also indispensable for the prevention of political corruption and the safeguarding of proper democratic procedures (on this see Etzioni-Halevy, 1983a). Democracy, itself a rather fragile institutional arrangement, is thus threatened and has already been rendered less democratic by various incongruous developments and internal contradictions.

Dye and Zeigler (1975) have convincingly made the point that the survival of democracy rests squarely on the shoulders of elites rather than on those of the people. It is the 'irony of democracy' that the elites, not the masses, have been most committed to democratic values, and have been the ones to safeguard democratic procedures. Presumably this includes the intellectual or Knowledge Elite as well. Yet this intellectual elite has been prominent only in pinpointing the threats to democracy. It (together with all other elites) has not been much help in showing the way towards protection against these threats to, and the inroads that have already been made into, democracy.

EXTERNAL PROBLEMS

No less worrying is another problem now facing Western society: the disparity between itself and the Third World. As is generally known, in the Third World millions suffer from undernourishment and its related diseases, while in the West millions suffer from overnourishment and *its* related diseases. For millions in the Third World undernourishment shades over into starvation, while in the West food is wilfully destroyed and farmers are paid to refrain from growing crops. And these are only the most extreme manifestations of the persistent gaps in economic development between the Third World and the West.[15] These gaps are morally disconcerting in their own right.

In addition, the bulk of the Third World is quite clearly yet another 'underclass' and there is no certainty that it will remain docile in that position. So far, of course, most of the Third World countries' upper classes and elites have not suffered (and may even have benefited) from the existent state of affairs, while the rural and urban lower classes have lacked the awareness or the power (or both) to instigate an effective revolt.

But more and more of the Third World's youth are now gaining a Western-style education, and with it an increasing consciousness of the gaps between their own countries and the West. Upon completing their education, many of them have no prospects of being absorbed into existent elites and into positions commensurate with their education and expectations, and cannot expect substantial benefits from the existent state of affairs.

Thus the possibility cannot be ruled out that they will spearhead collective action to signal their displeasure. Joining the Communist bloc (as Vietnam and Kampuchea, for instance, have done already) is one form such displeasure might take. In view of the accelerating spread of nuclear weapons, contemplating other forms that such signals might take amounts to thinking about the unthinkable.[16]

Intellectuals, and social scientists in particular, have not been oblivious to the gaps between the West and the Third World. Some scholars have attributed these gaps to the Third World countries' traditional norms and values and to many of their peoples' alleged lack of drive for achievement. They have thus blamed the Third World countries themselves for their underdevelopment. Other social scientists, especially of the neo-Marxist persuasion, have attributed these gaps to capitalist exploitation. According to their view, it is the contact between the capitalist West and the Third World which has brought development to the former and underdevelopment to the latter. The capitalist countries have forged ahead in economic development not only through the expropriation of surplus value from their own labouring classes, but also through expropriation of surplus from the Third World. They have done so (neo-Marxists claim) by distorting the Third World countries' agricultural production, by exploiting their cheap labour, and by generally restructuring their economies in line with Western (rather than Third World) needs.

But while intellectuals have been strong in constructing plausible (though mutually contradictory) theories on the causes of the gaps, they have achieved little or nothing in pointing the way towards their eradication. In their capacity as technocrats, many of them may have tried. But, to paraphrase Frank (1971), the ideas of intellectuals on underdevelopment have themselves been underdeveloped in their failure to contribute to the solution of the problem. And, once again, it is not that these ideas have not been influential. Just as intellectuals (as technocrats) have had a share in influencing

Western domestic policies, so too have they had a share in influencing Western policies towards developing countries.[17] In this area too, then, they (we) must accept a share of the blame for these policies' failure.

Most disquieting, of course, is the spiralling (conventional, nuclear, chemical and biological) arms race between the Western and communist blocs which not only brings the world closer to the brink of the unthinkable, but in the process swallows up enormous resources that could more fruitfully have served for the eradication of hunger and poverty. The role of the scientists whose knowledge serves as a basis for the development of armaments, and who are constantly in the process of perfecting their destructive capacity, will be dealt with later on. But intellectuals are indirectly connected with the problem in other capacities as well. Intellectuals are now staffing a number of eminent but completely innocuous peace research institutes. They are also involved in the problem on the level of policy. Just as they have been exerting a certain influence on other policy areas, so too has their so-called expertise been called upon in the areas of foreign and defence policy. Hence they (we) must also shoulder a certain part of the responsibility for the fact that the arms race is still forging ahead at full speed.

Whether or not these threats can be averted, and whether or not all other problems now coming to the fore in Western societies do, in fact, have solutions, is a moot question. Certainly they seem to have become more intractable recently. The fact is, however, that various types of intellectual have widely dispensed advice on how to reach such solutions. Moreover, several eminent scholars have legitimized this practice by creating the image of intellectuals as actually contributing towards these solutions. Hence the significance of the fact that intellectuals have recently proved to be as impotent in the face of these problems as politicians, bureaucrats and all other sections of the community.

WHEN PROPHECY FAILS

A significant section of the Knowledge Elite in Western society has been very much involved in forecasting the future. As Kumar (1978, pp. 185–6) comments, by the 1960s

> long range forecasting was . . . all the rage. Institutes of futurology proliferated in all the industrial societies of the world. Government and learned bodies set up 'think tanks' and commissions to produce reports and 'scenarios' on the future of their societies. There was the French Commissariat du Plan's '1985 Committee'; the Commission on the Year 2000 of the American Academy of Arts and Sciences; the British Social Science Research Council's Committee on the Next Thirty Three years (set up in 1967), the European-based *Futuribles* project, directed by Bertrand de Jouvenel, concerned with the commission of long-range predictions and projections in every area of society. A stream of books and symposia collections appeared with titles such as *The Year 2000, Mankind 2000, The World in 1984, Life in the Twenty-First Century, Future Shock, The Sociology of the Future*, even *The Future as an Academic Discipline*.

Like other parts of the Knowledge Elite, the scholars converging on the idea of the post-industrial society, too, have been concerned with predicting the future. As Kumar continues: ' "We have become oriented towards the future" declared the American sociologist Daniel Bell, Chairman of Commission of the Year 2000. "The future is on the agenda" was the more portentous pronouncement of futurologist Alvin Toffler.' And indeed, what post-industrialists had to say about what they termed the Knowledge Class in post-industrial society and about that society itself was based partly on their analysis of the existent situation and partly on the projection of existent trends into the future. But unfortunately some of the predicted trends of ever-greater abundance, equality, liberty and general well-being (see Chapter 3) subsequently reversed themselves or took off in the most unexpected directions, playing havoc with their predictions. To be sure, knowledge has been increasing in importance. But by now it should be abundantly clear that this knowledge has not been working in the manner visualized by the post-industrialists and recently has not helped increase the predicted prosperity, equity and freedom (or the viability of democracy) in Western society.

In the opening to his well-known book *Future Shock* (1970, p. 14), Toffler quotes an old Chinese proverb which says that 'to prophesy is extremely difficult – especially with respect to the future'. He then promptly proceeds to prophesy (or forecast) the future for the rest of the book. By now, with the hindsight provided by the events of the last decade, it should have become eminently clear that post-industrialists would have done well to heed the warning implied in the above old, but still very apt and appropriate, saying.

CONCLUSION

This chapter has presented a brief review of some of the mounting problems now facing Western society, to which the brilliant analyses of intellectuals have helped call our attention, but which the recently influential policy advice tendered by intellectuals has done nothing to alleviate. It was intended to substantiate the claim that this policy advice is much less than previously envisaged (especially by post-industrialists) the outgrowth of firmly based, relevant knowledge, and much more the outgrowth of uncertain gropings, in a generally groping society. It cannot be claimed that the policy advice dispensed by intellectuals has itself *created* these mounting problems. But it has been shown that these problems were mounting precisely when the intellectuals' policy advice was becoming more pervasive and influential. Hence intellectuals must face the claim that they, together with the other groups of people involved in the policy process (such as politicians and bureaucrats), have been implicated in the exacerbation of these problems.

Yet intellectuals (like Festinger's prophets) continue to act as if nothing had happened. They continue to be more adamant than ever in their belief in the fruitfulness of their knowledge, in the soundness of the advice emanating from that knowledge and in the salutary effects on policy emanating from that advice. Thereby intellectuals continue to legitimize grants of very substantial funds for applied social research on which much policy advice is subsequently based. Thereby they continue to justify the recently proliferating policy research institutes, think tanks, advisory committees, commissions of inquiry, consultantships and the like through which so many of their (our) numbers make or enhance their careers. Hence they continue to dispense policy advice as if the previously dispensed advice did in fact lead to the greater abundance, equality and freedom envisaged by post-industrialists.

The mounting socio-economic problems to which the policy advice tendered by the Knowledge Elite has probably contributed are among the causes for the recent squeeze on funding of the intellectual (or Knowledge) endeavour, in both academic and non-academic institutions, in both the private and the government sector. Thus, the Knowledge Elite has contributed, though indirectly and inadvertently, not only to the problems faced by Western society, but also to the problems it now faces itself. This funding squeeze, in turn, has led members of the Knowledge Elite to make even louder claims as to the beneficial results of their own endeavour. Thus intellectuals have been most vocal in their self-justification precisely when the problems in whose aggravation they (together with other influential groups in society) have been implicated have become most prominent.

NOTES: CHAPTER 4

1 For instance, the proportion of people aged 65 and over in Britain was 10·8 per cent in 1951 and 15 per cent in 1978; in the USA it was 8·2 per cent in 1950 and 11·2 per cent in 1979; in France it was 11·5 per cent in 1954 and 14 per cent in 1979.

2 The percentage of single-parent families (as defined in official statistics) grew in the USA from 6·2 in 1970 to 10·4 in 1981 and in Australia from 5 in 1966 to 8·8 in 1975 (Etzioni-Halevy, 1983b).

3 In the USA unemployment went down from 10·4 per cent of the workforce in February 1983 to 7·4 per cent in February 1985 (as against less than 5 per cent in the 1950s and 1960s). In Britain unemployment went down from 14·8 per cent of the workforce in January 1983 to 13 per cent of the work-force in February 1985 (as against less than 3 per cent in the 1950s and 1960s).

4 Compiled and computed from *Statistical Abstract of the United States, 1982–3*, table 1, p. 6; table 529, p. 326; table 553, pp. 338–9; *Social Indicators – 3*, table 8/5, p. 397. See also report in *The Australian*, 27 July 1983.

5   Thus in the USA such expenditures have risen from 8 per cent of GNP in
    1970 to 13·3 per cent in 1983. And in Great Britain they have risen from
    20·5 per cent of GNP in 1970 to 25·5 per cent in 1980 (see Etzioni-Halevy,
    1983b).

6   See *Australian Financial Review*, 30 December 1983, p. 5.

7   Thus total tax receipts – as percentage of GDP – in the UK were 29·8 in
    1955 and 35·9 in 1980; in the USA they were 23·6 in 1955 and 30·7 in 1980;
    and in West Germany they were 30·8 per cent in 1955 and 37·2 per cent in
    1980 (Etzioni-Halevy, 1983a, p. 118).

8   For a review of these and similar data see Etzioni-Halevy, 1981, pp. 131–5.

9   In Britain, for instance, the top 1 per cent of the population owned 23 per
    cent of all marketable wealth in 1980 (*Social Trends*, 1983, p. 78). In the
    USA the top 2·5 per cent of the population own 39 per cent of the country's
    wealth, while the bottom 50 per cent of the population own no more than 4
    per cent of that wealth.

    Figures recently released by the Australian Bureau of Statistics show that
    in 1981–2 the bottom 10 per cent of income-earners received 1·9 per cent of
    all income compared with 2·7 per cent in 1978–9 and 3·2 per cent in
    1973–4. Concomitantly the share of the top 10 per cent of income-earners
    increased from 22·2 per cent in 1973–4 to 27·8 per cent in 1978–9 and to 29
    per cent in 1981–2.

    In the USA the income ratio for the highest to the lowest fifth of families
    was 7·2 in 1966 but 7·6 in 1976. From 1976 to 1978 the median real income
    of the highest fifth of families was still rising while that of the lowest fifth
    was not, thus further increasing the gap between them. *Statistical Abstract
    of the United States*, 1980, table 752, p. 454.

10 See note 3 above.

11 It is exceedingly difficult to establish the threshold of poverty objectively.
    All that can be said is that the poor live close to, or below, generally
    accepted subsistence standards. The criterion certainly applies to those
    forced to subsist on unemployment benefits.

12 *Statistical Abstract of the United States*, 1982–3, p. 441.

13 See Gans, 1973; Kincaid, 1973; Liebow, 1967; Miliband, 1974;
    Westergaard and Resler, 1976; and several others.

14 Periodically statistics appear purporting to show that income inequalities
    in communist countries are smaller than in Western countries. These
    statistics, however, are not very meaningful as they do not take into account
    the various perquisites accruing to members of elites and higher-ranking
    occupations in those countries (including special housing, dachas,
    limousines, special schools for their children, special hospitals and medical
    care arrangements, special shops selling scarce products, etc.) and setting
    them completely apart from the 'masses'.

15 Average annual growth of GNP per capita from 1960 to 1976 was 0·9 per
    cent in low-income developing countries, 2·8 per cent in middle-income
    developing countries and 3·4 per cent in industrialized Western countries.
    By 1976 GNP per capita in US dollars was 150 in low-income developing
    countries, 750 in middle-income developing countries and 6,200 in
    Western industrialized countries (see World Bank, 1978, pp. 76–7).

16 This, of course, is the title of Herman Kahn's book on nuclear war (1962).

17 On this see, for instance, Chirot, 1977, ch. 1.

Part Three

ILLUSTRATIONS

5

The Poverty of the Economist

In 1846 Pierre Proudhon wrote a treatise entitled *The Philosophy of Poverty*. In response, Karl Marx wrote a book of his own, entitled *The Poverty of Philosophy* (first published in 1847), in which he summarily attacked Proudhon's work. Had Marx still been alive today, it is not inconceivable that he might have written another book entitled *The Poverty of Economics* or, even more appropriately, *The Poverty of the Economist*. In this chapter I argue that a title such as this would certainly have been topical today.

In the last chapter the poverty of the Knowledge Elite, of intellectuals, was discussed in general terms and intellectuals were dealt with as a composite group. In this and the following chapter some of the arguments presented before are illustrated with respect to concrete categories of intellectuals, beginning with economists.

The discussion of economists and of their discipline here is meant to illustrate the argument (presented in Chapter 3) that the creation of theoretical knowledge in the humanities and social sciences and the formation of policy fundamentally diverge from each other, that bridging the gap between them is exceedingly difficult, and that this has become especially evident in recent years.

Economists and economics are singled out for such a discussion because of the especially high regard in which they have been held and because of the massive impact they have had on policy and politics in modern Western society. Because of these, much has come to be expected of economists, and the disappointment resulting from their inability to live up to those expectations must be that much greater.

As G. Barker (1982, p. 11) writes,

> The trouble with economics ... is essentially that its
> practitioners and their theories have been elevated to a status
> which they cannot justify. To be an economist is, to many
> people, to be a combination of high priest, guru and
> soothsayer; it is to possess a passkey to the secrets of the
> future.

In other words an economist is, to many people, what I have
called a prophet. In turn I would argue that the economists'
status as proclaimed prophets rests on three presumed bases. It
rests on their discipline being widely regarded as a science. It
rests on their consequent perceived ability to discover laws and
hence predict (or forecast) the future. It rests, finally, on the
economists' perceived capacity to control the economy and
hence to tender advice that will lead to a maximization of
economic growth and to a minimization of economic problems,
crises and recessions. Their status as prophets thus rests on their
perceived capacity to guide society to a more affluent future. In
recent years, however, it has become increasingly clear (or
should have) that all three presumptions are dubious.

THE POVERTY OF THE ECONOMIST AS SCIENTIST

The status of economists as proclaimed prophets derives in part
from their discipline being regarded as a science. The economist
is thus popularly presumed to possess a very special and
authoritative type of knowledge. In some circles this is
presumed to be the type of knowledge which, if not based on
divine revelation, is the next best thing to it. But a closer look at
the actual situation shows that the economist is but a poor
scientist.

The poverty of the economist as scientist rests on the poverty
of economics as science. As Barker (1982) continues in his
above-mentioned critique, economics holds itself out to be a
science, that is, a discipline that generates general explanatory
and/or predictive models about the way society reacts to
different sorts of stimuli. If you understand these models you

can explain/predict what is going to happen. In fact, economics has not done well as a science, especially at the macro level:

> it has failed to agree about how the economy works and why it works as it does. Even the most sophisticated computer models of the economy are grounded on theories, on sets of law-like statements that are untestable ... They are, therefore, of dubious explanatory or predictive power. (Barker, 1982, p. 11)

Barker then goes on to quote the American philosopher of science, Daniel M. Hausman (1981, p. 27), who writes:

> Since the eighteenth century, many economists have believed that, given reasonably favorable conditions, self-interested voluntary exchanges lead to coherent and efficient economic organization. Yet the theories which economists have possessed have not enabled them to explain how this order in fact comes about nor even to show how it is possible that such order could come about. Economic theorists might thus reasonably be in doubt concerning both whether their theoretical framework captures the crucial features of the economy and whether it is likely to lead them to an adequate theory.

A similar statement has been made by H. S. Katz (1976, p. 62) to the effect that

> Modern economics claims to be a science. This is a sham and a fraud. It has all of the outer paraphernalia of science and none of its essence. It ostentatiously flaunts mathematical symbols (such as the supply and demand functions) and formulae ($MV = PT$) without any real understanding of what these things are. When it fails to predict future events (an occurrence of continual embarrassment to modern economists), it does not act like the scientist, disregarding false theories in search of the truth; it acts like the Indian Medicine Man who has failed to make rain. It equivocates, rationalizes and tries to make minor adjustments.

Mathematical symbols used in economics are often considered scientific and rigorous. 'This is nonsense on stilts', remarks G. Withers (1984, p. 5). Quantification of economic entities is often considered as a tool for empirical testing of various paradigmatically derived theories. In fact, however, econometrics can only provide usable estimates within one economic paradigm. Most economic theorists avoid close comparisons between theories from alternative paradigms. But even when the comparison is made econometrics cannot serve as an empirical basis for choosing between such alternative theories.

This holds for economics in general, too. Or in D. Clark's (1983a, p. 12) words, contrary to the procedure in science, in economics

There are no shoot-outs after which the vanquished theory is laid to rest. Instead it is more a situation of shooting at an ever moving target, with theories reappearing once again from behind the shooting gallery hall, perhaps dented a little but still erect.

Of course, in this respect economics is not unique. It merely falls in line with its sister disciplines such as sociology and the study of politics which sometimes have been tempted to present themselves not merely as scholarly disciplines but as sciences in the full sense of the term. Certainly they have not been more justified than economics in doing so. However, economics is unique in that it has not only presented itself as a science but has been more widely accepted as such by the community as well as by political and bureaucratic policy-makers. It is for this reason that the policy advice tendered by its representatives has been regarded as well founded and it is for this reason that this advice (much more than the advice given by sociologists, for instance) has often been followed and has widely permeated policies (and politics) in contemporary Western societies.

As noted, however, what actually happens in economics has only a faint resemblance to scientific procedure. We saw earlier (in Chapter 3) that even in the natural and physical sciences theories are not conclusively refuted by any particular piece of empirical evidence. Nevertheless, when sufficient inconsistencies, new problems and new data accumulate which together throw a theory into doubt, it is eventually replaced by a new one. Not so in economics. Here, as old theories are never discarded and superseded by new ones, and as they therefore periodically pop up again, it is not surprising that various contradictory theories co-exist within the discipline. The problem is less in micro-economics, where most economists adhere to the neo-classical school of thought. But in macro-economics there are fundamental, ongoing controversies among economists with regard to different theories' validity and fruitfulness as well as their ability to withstand the test of time. This is not to say that some of these theories do not afford valuable insights into the economy. But the persistent controversies surrounding them necessarily raise questions with respect to their scientific status.

Today, besides the time-honoured controversy between Marxist economists and others, the most basic and pervasive controversy seems to be that between the followers of John Maynard Keynes or the Keynesians on the one hand, and the followers of Milton Friedman or the neo-classical monetarists on the other hand. As this controversy is usually presented, it was Keynes's view that the 'invisible hand' (which Adam Smith and his followers had believed in) was not sufficient to regulate a modern economy. Rather, he saw government intervention as both appropriate and necessary, especially in a recession when the economy was not producing full employment and growth. Further, it was his view that, at least in a non-inflationary environment, an expansionary monetary and fiscal government policy was likely to pull the economy out of recession. Freidman's alternative conception, for its part, was a reformulated version of pre-Keynesian, classical economics. Friedman saw inflation as the root of all evil, believed that this evil was itself caused by an excessive growth in money supply, hence advocated the strict non-discretionary control of that supply in conjunction with a free market economy.

Keynes's views reigned supreme for some decades and in particular in the 1950s and 1960s. But with the 1973/4 economic downturn and the resultant economic instability, the reputation of successful economic management with the aid of Keynesian economics began to recede and free market monetarism (supported by the rise of the New Right in countries such as Britain, the United States and Australia) began to rear its head. As Sir John Mason[1] remarked (see Lunn, 1983, p. 4): 'And lo, the prophet Keynes was found wanting. But the new prophet appeared – Professor Friedman, a prophet who didn't have a god but who had a devil: the devil of inflation.'

Richard Nixon once said 'We are all Keynesians now'. Ironically he made this remark 'just as [many] economists were falling over themselves to disown the doctrines of Lord Keynes for those of Milton Friedman' (Potts, 1983, p. 9). Something similar now seems to be happening to Friedman's doctrines, thus apparently swinging the pendulum at least partly back towards Keynes. An Oxford economist, D. Hendry, and his associate N. Ericsson, in a brief paper, have allegedly destroyed the empirical evidence on which Friedman's monetarist theory was based 'brick by crumbling brick' (Huhne, 1983). Even so, the controversy between the followers of the two masters has not been resolved, and each school of thought seems to believe that not only scientific validity, but salvation too, lies on its own side; which to an outsider seems to indicate that salvation lies on neither side. With every renewed controversy between economists it seems to move further and further away.

Keynes's most famous and most frequently quoted statement is undoubtedly that 'in the long run we are all dead'. Strange as it may seem, however, even this seemingly indisputable statement has raised some controversy. As Friedman (1983) noted, the context in which this statement was made was a discussion on how changes in the quantity of money would, in the short run, affect the velocity of output and prices, though in the long run the effect would be on prices only. 'But', Keynes (1971, p. 65) went on, 'this *long run* is a misleading guide to current affairs' for '*In the long run* we are all dead. Economists set themselves too easy, too useless a task if in tempestuous seasons they can only tell us that when the storm is long past, the ocean is flat again.'

Friedman's own reaction to this statement was that Keynes

'tended to neglect the cumulative effect of short-run policies. The truth that in the long run we are all dead needs to be balanced by the equally relevant truth that the long run consists of a succession of short runs.' And as even Keynes's most straightforward and popular statement was challenged this has continued to be the case, and even more so, with regard to his more complex ideas.

Moreover, to an outsider it would seem that economists are not only unable to agree on whether Keynes's theory has any scientific validity and on whether it has withstood the test of time. It seems, rather, that economists are also unable to agree on what Keynes's theory actually was. As Potts (1983, p. 9) put it, 'The question arises whether Keynes really meant what people think he said, or whether whatever it was he said was wrong . . . The debate is still unresolved because Keynes was such a prodigious author, virtually writing something for everyone.' Hence the feeling has frequently been expressed that 'The answer to our economic problems today must surely be buried somewhere in the writings of Keynes, if only we knew which one', Friedman 'argued that Keynes was both misunderstood and wrong but even he [i.e. Friedman] failed to knock Keynes off his pedestal. Indeed, Keynes is coming back into favor. It is no longer proper to criticize him; instead you have to re-interpret what Keynes said to suit your own argument.'

Consequently, economic thought today is divided not only between Keynesians and monetarists but between different interpreters of Keynes, that is, between different types of Keynesians. As Potts continues,

> The Keynesians can be divided according to their views on real wages. Those who think real wages do not matter are usually called Keynesians; whereas those who believe real wages are important are the real proponents of Keynes, even if many do not realize it . . . Real wages are the salient distinction because Keynesians want an incomes policy combined with more spending. Crypto-Keynesians would reduce real wages and possibly government spending.

To paraphrase Nixon's previously cited statement, it would

seem, then, that many of us are born-again Keynesians today, though of different shapes and brands.

Some of the rest of us, it would seem, are still monetarists (albeit, perhaps, in shrinking numbers) and this school of thought too is divided internally. Indeed, the initiated seem to be able to identify no less than five distinct brands of monetarism, whose proponents are in constant controversy not only with Keynesians but with each other as well. In addition, a new group of non-monetarist neo-classical economists, supply siders, institutional economists, ecletic economists and Marxist or neo-Marxist political economists have also been identified (Withers, 1978) and these too are constantly embattled with each other.

It would seem, further, that all this incestuous infighting adds to the confusion rife in economics, so that for an outsider to find his/her way in this discipline a guide for the perplexed would be needed. Not surprisingly, that outsider would find it rather difficult to accord this embattled discipline the status of a science.

The claim of economics to scientific validity is also tarnished, among other reasons because of its sometimes rather dubious way of building models. In this connection an anecdote popular among sociologists tells of an expedition of three scholars, a physicist, a geologist and an economist, stranded in a remote desert. The only sustenance they had left was a can of beans, but nothing with which to open it. The physicist suggested that his spectacles be used as lenses through which the sun's rays would be focused on the can, so that a hole would be pierced in it. The geologist proposed that a sharp rock be used to achieve the same effect. And the economist said: 'First, let's assume a can opener . . .' It seems that in building their economic models, many economists rely on equally unwarranted assumptions. In particular, they rely on the assumption that all relevant[2] economic actors are rational, imbued with perfect knowledge of all relevant circumstances and an unceasing desire to maximize the benefits of all their relevant actions.

Clark (1983a, p. 12) pointed out that one of the great novelties of Keynes's *General Theory* was his insistence that most of our positive actions spring from spontaneous optimism rather than from rational expectations, as he wrote: 'Most probably, our decisions to do something positive, the full consequences of which will be drawn out over many days to come, can only be taken as a result of animal spirits and not as the outcome of a weighted average of quantitative benefits multiplied by quantitative probabilities.' But many of his followers ignored this less developed side of Keynes and they (together with other contemporary economists) have been unperturbed in their reliance on crude, rationalist assumptions with regard to economically relevant action and actors. Although they have been dealing with human beings, they have supplied ample and continuous evidence of 'the poorly developed psychological side of economic modelling' (loc. cit). And since economic models have frequently been based on unwarranted assumptions, it is not surprising that they have frequently come up with unwarranted conclusions.

As a consequence of all this there has recently been a growing realization, even among economists themselves, of the limitations of all economic model building – be it Keynesian, monetarist, or any other brand. If this is so, then the continuous debate among economists may not have been in vain. For as Clark (ibid., p. 13) formulates the idea: 'There has been a very important and positive result of all the disputation. We now know a lot more about the limitations of the competing theories and of the models . . . used to support them.' Let us, then, keep this knowledge in mind in evaluating the economists' advice with respect to policies on which so much of our welfare and well-being depends.

THE POVERTY OF THE ECONOMIST AS PROPHET

Since economics has been widely regarded as a science and economists as scientists, they have popularly been thought to have discovered the scientific laws which govern modern economies. As a consequence they have also been presumed to be able to apply the knowledge of such general laws to forecast the economic future. In fact, nothing could be further from the truth, and economists have not been any more successful as forecasters than they have been as scientists.

Earlier in the book reference was made to the Popperian distinction between conditional predictions ('if x then y'), typically made by exact scientists, and prophecies ('y will occur'), typically produced by social scientists. Subsequently it could be seen that many social scientists have indeed put the future on their agendas and hence produced large series of such prophecies. In this respect economists are in line with what social scientists in general have been doing, as they too have attempted to gaze into the future and produce prophecies in the Popperian sense (see illustrations below).

In producing such prophecies economists act very much as intellectuals by our definition since, using their discipline as a basis, they develop and present a certain body of ideas. And as is the case with other types of intellectual endeavours, here too there is a major cleavage between ideas and practice – in this case between the forecasts and what actually happens. And since many economic forecasts are not borne out in practice it is not surprising that policy advice emanating from such forecasts is of little practical benefit to policy-makers.

The most important economic developments of the last few decades have been the economic setbacks and recessions of the 1970s, beginning with the marked economic downturn of 1973/4. Yet beforehand (with the exception of some Marxists who had been predicting doom on the basis of their general theory of capitalism) economists had no inkling of what was to eventuate. And when the recession came it caught them unawares. As Draper (1977, p. 60) summarized the situation in America:

> When [intellectuals] first invaded the government . . . they were filled with self-confidence. The economists forged into the lead . . . By 1973, the economists again led the way – in retreat. That year the new President of the American Economic Association, Professor Walter Heller, spoke for the profession when he said: . . . The energy crisis caught us with our parameters down.

This is best exemplified by the OECD economic forecasts for the second part of 1973 and for 1974 as published in the *OECD*

Economic Outlook of July 1973 (p. 13). This forecast, under the heading 'Domestic Prospects', runs as follows:

> *The growth of output in the OECD area is expected to reach an almost unprecedented 7 to 7½ per cent rate this year ...* Some deceleration is now expected in the growth of output from the exceptionally rapid pace recorded over the last 18 months, *but above-capacity rates of expansion are still likely in most Member countries into 1974.*

Current boom

> The Secretariat's forecasts for GNP growth to mid-1974 ... suggest that the boom at present underway may be strongest [*sic*] witnessed by the area as a whole since the early 1950s. Output growth is expected to remain at, or above, a seasonally adjusted annual rate of 6½ per cent through 1973, following a full year (1972) of similar strength. Some deceleration is, however, expected to set in early next year, notably in the United States and Germany. The upswing, which in 1972 was still concentrated in North America, appears at present to be broadly based with hardly any European Member country expected to grow at less than 5 per cent through 1973 and into 1974.

A year later, however, it became clear that developments had been precisely the opposite from those predicted.

In the *OECD Economic Outlook* of July 1974 (p. 9), once more under the heading 'Domestic Prospects', OECD economists had to admit that

> *The OECD area has just gone through the most exceptional deceleration of growth ever experienced.* For the seven major countries combined, growth of real GNP in the first half of 1973 was at about 8 per cent per annum; the latest available indicators suggest that output fell in the first half of 1974, probably at an annual rate of 1½ per cent, with most countries participating in the deceleration. (Italics added)

The contrast between the predicted and the actual economic

growth in major OECD countries during the first half of 1974 can be gleaned from Table 5.1

Table 5.1   *Growth of Real Gross National Product in Seven Major OECD Countries during the First Half of 1974 (percentage changes seasonally adjusted at annual rates)*

	July 1973 Forecast	Actual Developments
Canada	$5\frac{3}{4}$	6
United States	$4\frac{1}{2}$	$-2\frac{3}{4}$
Japan	$10\frac{1}{2}$	$-6\frac{1}{2}$
France[a]	6	$4\frac{3}{4}$
Germany	$5\frac{1}{2}$	2
Italy	$5\frac{1}{4}$	$2\frac{1}{2}$
United Kingdom[b]	$4\frac{1}{2}$	-6
Total of above countries	$5\frac{1}{2}$	$-1\frac{1}{2}$

Sources: OECD Economic Outlook, no. 13, July 1973, p. 13, table 1; and no. 15, July 1974, p. 9, table 1.
Notes:
[a] GDP.
[b] 1970 weights and exchange rates.

Economists may thus be good at forecasting when existent trends continue. But when the unusual happens and trends are reversed they are as baffled and confounded as the rest of us.

A similar phenomenon may be illustrated by OECD economic forecasts made in the last few years concerning real growth in Gross Domestic Product of its member countries. As can be seen from Figure 5.1, in two out of three years the forecasts were by far too optimistic and things turned out rather differently in reality. In particular, the OECD forecasters were taken by surprise by the depth of the 1982 slump, a 0·5 per cent fall in real GDP, compared with earlier forecasts of a 2 per cent growth.

Such excessive (or at least premature) optimism may also be illustrated by another (though less dramatic) off-the-mark economic forecast. In July 1983 the then Secretary to the Australian Treasury, John Stone, engaged in an economic debate with an American visiting economist, Nobel Prize winner Professor Lawrence Klein. In the course of the argument Mr Stone reminded Professor Klein that fifteen months previously, in March 1982, US Secretary to the Treasury Donald Regan had stated (no doubt on the basis of the forecasts from his department's economists) that the American economy was about to 'come out roaring like a bull'. Professor Klein had to confess that 'those predictions were somewhat astray', but he added that the recovery had arrived a couple of quarters later (Bowden, 1983).

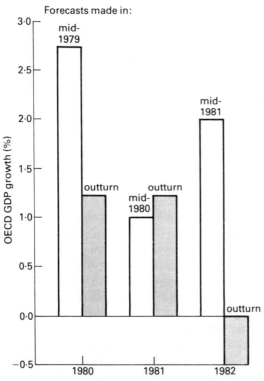

Figure 5.1   *Growth in real Gross Domestic Product in all OECD countries.*
Source: The Economist, 14 May 1983, p. 118.

In connection with forecasts such as these, Samuelson (1983, p. 16) has this to say: 'In truth our forecasts are too boringly similar. And what we agree on is this, that our last consensus was wrong and is to be replaced by the new one.'

Once economists have reached this conclusion, they then seek to rationalize and justify their previous forecasting failures; and having rationalized away those failures, they subsequently continue their forecasting unperturbed. This can be seen, for instance, from the most recent OECD publications where (as in previous publications) forecast follows forecast in rapid succession. Thus economists are surprisingly similar in their forecasting behaviour to the (previously discussed) prophets analysed by Festinger and his colleagues, whose inevitable failures have led to an unperturbed continuation of prophetic activities.

THE POVERTY OF THE ECONOMIST IN MANAGING CRISES

A prominent economist is reported to have held a learned discourse on various options for market investments. At the end of the lecture, upon soliciting questions, he was confronted with the following: 'Dear Professor so-and-so. If you're so smart, why aren't you rich?' Allegorically, the same question may be asked of Western economists collectively. If these economists are so smart, why have not the Western economies, which have had the benefit of their analysis and advice, been in better shape in recent years?

Until recently it was a common truism that economists had learned to cope with economic crises, that like the mythical, primeval flood reported in the Old Testament, the 1929 crash and the subsequent Depression could never happen again. Today, on the other hand, we are no longer sure. We continue to hope, of course, that these events will not recur. But following the trends of the last decade, the sudden slowdown, arrest and even reversal of economic growth (as summarized in Table 5.2), we have less confidence in the economists' ability to prevent them from doing so.

In this context it is interesting to note that Keynes was, in fact, not only smart but quite rich as well, and that he had obtained his riches through propitious investments. (Although by some accounts, his investments were made in the commodity market on which he claimed no special expertise.) But the question of whether he had a positive effect on the Western economy is still open to debate.

Table 5.2   *Average Annual Percentage Rate of Change of Real GDP per capita in OECD Countries, 1960–82*

	All OECD Countries	OECD Europe	EEC Countries
1960–67	3·9	3·5	3·5
1967–73	3·9	4·2	4·3
1973–80	1·7	1·7	2·0
1981	1·2	–0·3	–0·6
1982	–0·4	0·3	0·1

Sources: OECD Economic Outlook – Historical Statistics 1960–1980 (Paris), 1982, s. 3, table 3.2, p. 4; *OECD Economic Outlook*, no. 32, December 1982, table 2, p. 16; *OECD Main Economic Indicators*, June 1983, p. 180.

Keynes did see the Great Depression as a problem that could and must be resolved by human action. As he saw it, 'The invisible hand was arthritic and had dropped its bundle' (Clark, 1983b, p. 35). Thus good minds, including his own, ought to be turned to producing a more humane economic situation. But did he, in fact, help do so?

Recently it has been argued that there never was a Keynesian solution to the Great Depression. In the United States, initially, the government pursued a restrictive monetary policy, entailing raised interest rates and diminished investments. According to this view, even the New Deal policy (introduced to counter the Depression) did not have the desired effect. Right through the mid-1930s the government policy aimed at a balanced budget. Moreover, according to this view, even towards the later 1930s, when United States economic policy came to be based on Keynesian-type theories, this did not make much of a difference. Indeed, it is widely believed (though Samuelson, 1983, for one disagrees) that the Depression only receded through the preparations for war which led to full employment.

With regard to Britain, Sir John Mason recently commented

that between 1931 and 1937 the government 'was a highly orthodox balanced-budget, sound-money government, and the investment which caused British industrial production to go up in those years by 50 per cent and the Gross National Product by 25 per cent was private investment'. Thus there never was a Keynesian solution to the Depression, 'yet this illusion was nurtured in the '50s and '60s . . . when times were good and we really did think as our standard of living went up – that we had found a solution to world economic problems' (see Lunn, 1983, p. 4).

It is during this same timespan that Keynesian economics did, in fact, succeed. This in itself was no mean achievement. And most economists have relied on the postwar full employment experience as their evidence for thirty years of Keynesian effectiveness.

The 1970s thus came to many as a rude awakening and as the shattering of a cherished illusion. For during this period we learned that not only could recession follow recession without the economists being able to show the way out, but even now, when the recession itself is receding (at least for the time being), the economists seem as perplexed as the rest of us as to why this is happening. All they seem able to offer are partial, *post factum* explanations for the recession, and no one seems to claim with any degree of seriousness that the economists are the ones to be pulling us out of it.

As Sir John Mason, himself an economist, concludes (ibid.):

Our society today has five . . . perceptions about recessions – we know when they are coming, we know what causes them, we know how to alleviate them, we know when they are going away, and we think governments [upon the advice of economists] can do something about them. All these perceptions are false. [In fact, we do not know] in any way how to control our economies, [we do not] have the skill, the knowledge, or the power, to significantly alter the economic circumstances.

This, moreover, is true in more general terms as well: 'A thousand Lord Keynes in the [British] Treasury since the war would have made no difference to the post-war performance of the British economy – the problems are not resolvable by intellectual horsepower.'

Perhaps this would explain the statement of Joe Haines (who was Prime Minister Harold Wilson's press secretary and close adviser for several years) concerning the economists of the British Treasury:

> with a certainty which successive Chancellors have invariably mistaken for wisdom, these financial Fu Manchus have presided over, nurtured, cosseted and brought to flower almost every kind of economic crisis ... they managed to achieve the worst unemployment since the war, deflation and inflation, recession, rising prices and falling living standards, and all at once, and yet their supremacy is rarely challenged. (Haines, 1977, pp. 40–1)

It has sometimes been argued that the fault lies not with the economists but with the policy-makers who have been loath to accept their advice. Especially when the medicine for crises prescribed by economists is bitter-tasting, the patients have preferred to leave it on the shelf. But this argument is rebutted by the fact that (as seen before) economists are so divided among themseves as to be unable to agree on the proper prescription.

This brings us back to the fact that although the recession may presently be receding (whether permanently or temporarily no one is able to tell), this development can hardly be attributed to the salubrious advice tendered by economists. This, too, is so because the recommendations offered by different economists (just like the theories on which they are based) are significantly different from each other. This leaves policy-makers, even when keen to accept the economists' advice, at a loss to know which advice to accept.

This is well illustrated by a mini-survey, conducted by the Australian magazine *The Bulletin* at the beginning of 1983 among six top economists, on how to get the sluggish Australian economy moving again. Table 5.3 summarizes their replies.

Table 5.3 *Six Paths to Salvation*

	D. Stammer	H. Bell	N. Norman	D. Ironmonger	D. Harrison	F. Gruen
No. 1 problem/ priority?	Move slowly	Don't rock boat	Attack inflation	Create jobs	Restrain wages	Full employment improved balance of payments
Acceptable deficit?	$7bn–$8bn	Should be restrained	About $6bn	Not important issue	$4bn	No bigger than now
Moderate wages?	Yes	Through consensus	Yes	Through prices, incomes policy	Yes	It is central
Stimulate economy?	No	No	No	Yes	No	Yes, but carefully

The Bulletin, 5 April 1983, p. 22.

Advice that pay rises be moderated was the nearest thing to a common thread among the economists' recommendations. In all other respects their advice differed widely. At one end of the scale the advice was to fight inflation first; at the other end it was suggested that first the economy needs to be stimulated. In the middle, the counsel was not to do too much at all. Thus, whichever path the Australian government eventually follows, it must necessarily fit the advice of some economist and be contrary to the advice of other economists.

This also brings us back to the fact that the now-waning recession is leaving behind a rather unpleasant legacy, that of relatively high unemployment. Although in some Western countries unemployment has recently declined, in several countries the rates of unemployment are now nearly half as high as they were during the Great Depression[3] (as against less than 5 per cent unemployment in the same countries in the postwar era).

Moreover, while unemployment started to climb during (and presumably partly because of) the recession, economists now tell us that overcoming the recession cannot be expected to lead to overcoming unemployment, that multitudes of jobs are gone, never to return. Of course, economists may be wrong in this forecast as they have been in previous ones. However, we are now authoritatively told that we cannot expect unemployment to revert to the erstwhile low levels of the 1950s and 1960s. This, we are told, is due to the level and structure of welfare benefits and wages. It is also due, we are told, to growing automation and computerization in industry and in all other economic and work-related activities. And for this, the economists claim, they are not to be blamed. But so far economists have purported to be able to devise economic policies that would check unemployment whatever its source. It now becomes gradually evident that this is no longer the case.

'The economy must be stimulated with public works programmes', cry the Keynesians; 'Oh, no, that would create some jobs in the short term, but would bring higher inflation roaring back and soon destroy not just those jobs but others', cry the monetarists. (Smark, 1982)

Sadly, however, the battle of the theories is of little help in the battle against unemployment. Indeed, many economists no longer have realistic hopes of achieving a considerable reduction in unemployment, and some apparently no longer see their task as trying to achieve such a reduction. As one French economic planner reportedly put it rather bluntly: 'Our task now is to make people understand that unemployment is here to stay.'[4]

And yet unemployment has really been the aspect of the recession to cause the most human misery, hopelessness and despair. If economic recovery is not to lead to substantial employment recovery, the economic crisis will merely be replaced by a jobs crisis in which many in our midst will be left as badly off as they were before. If all economists can presently do is to make people understand that this is in fact the case, their success in managing the problems of modern Western economies can hardly be regarded as overwhelming.

CONCLUSION

Economists provide a prominent example of intellectuals or members of the Knowledge Elite whose elegant and impressive theoretical models recently have not been matched by impressive practical contributions to society. In the framework of the discipline with which they work and which they create and recreate, Western economists have proved themselves to be neither reliable forecasters of the future state of the economy nor yet able to manage and control economic crises and recessions. And this double failure has become especially prominent in recent years. It is therefore difficult to feel confident when economists have a major say in shaping the policies on which society's economic well-being depends. Seemingly, the only conclusion that can be reached is (to paraphrase Friedman, 1983, p. 8) that the economy is much too serious a matter to be left to the economists. But we do not have much choice; everyone else knows even less about it.

NOTES: CHAPTER 5

The idea for the title of this chapter comes from an article entitled 'The poverty of economics' by G. Barker, *The Age*, 20 November 1982.

1 The then British High Commissioner to Australia.
2 Most economic 'laws' (e.g. on supply and demand) only require that there be a sufficient margin of economically rational persons who respond in the way assumed. The constraint on the others is not that they cannot be driven by other motives. Rather, it is that these do not lead them to respond 'perversely' to economic changes, for instance, buy more if prices rise and nothing else has changed. (I am grateful to Dr G. Withers of The Australian National University for making this point.)
3 Sweden and Japan, with rates of unemployment of 4 per cent and 2·4 per cent respectively, are among the few countries that have managed to keep unemployment down.
4 Reported in the *Sydney Morning Herald*, 25 October 1982.

6

The Scientist Giveth and the Scientist Taketh Away

Ever since its inception, and in particular since the Enlightenment, modern science has been associated in Western thought with progress. Advancing scientific knowledge, especially in the physical and natural sciences, has been regarded as a value in its own right. In addition, it was intended to be used to control and harness nature in the service of humanity. Scientists creating that knowledge were to be the ones to make such progress possible. Unlike some economists and other social scientists, physical and natural scientists have not usually been presented and have not usually presented themselves as forecasters of the future. But the notion has become prevalent (and scientists have done little to dispel it) that their task, like that of the prophet, is to help guide society towards a better future.

In some ways the natural and physical (or exact) scientists have, in fact, been living up to these expectations. In contrast to economists and other social scientists, these physical and natural scientists have created disciplines that have indeed been advancing, at least in some areas and to some extent, through the discarding of outmoded theories and their replacement by more fruitful ones. Despite what some of the more extreme 'relativist' philosophers of science are now claiming (see Chapter 3), I would still maintain that the natural sciences have generated more rapidly progressing disciplines than the social sciences can ever hope to be.

While undergoing progress, these sciences have also engendered progress for society in the areas of the health, affluence and longevity of its members. The scientists who have created this knowledge have therefore made a substantial contribution to the welfare of modern society. We clearly owe them a debt of gratitude. For their contribution scientists have been justly rewarded with honours and high-ranking positions. Perhaps we owe them even greater honours and emoluments than have so far accrued to them.

. . . AND TAKETH AWAY

Unfortunately, however, the scientist, like the Lord, giveth and taketh away. In other words, as is becoming widely recognized today, the effects of scientific knowledge on society are not only benign but harmful as well. And the harmful effects of the knowledge the scientists have produced now confront us in the form of socio-political problems whose solutions, at this time, seem rather remote.

To be sure, scientists have not intended to create those problems and in many cases have not foreseen that they would occur. The problems have been, rather, the unanticipated consequences of the solutions they have devised for previous problems. Nevertheless, the problems are now there. And although they have had their origin in the realm of science, they have clear socio-political ramifications. And although they have been created by scientists, it is society at large which must now cope with them.

HOW SCIENCE CREATES PROBLEMS

Earlier in the book it was argued that the noxious no less than the salubrious effects of science are not incidental by-products but inherent in the very nature of science itself. Is this indeed the case? It has lately been claimed that the relationship between science and technology or between scientific knowledge and practical applications is more roundabout than was previously thought (see Chapter 3) and that credit (or blame) for many innovations should go to technology rather than to science. But the attempt to portion out credit between science and technology for innovations is frequently hampered by the lack of commonly agreed definitions. It can easily be shown that many innovations derive from research aimed at practical problem-solving. Hence when only pure research, prompted by intellectual curiosity, is recognized as a scientific endeavour, a gap between science and technology is easily visible. But if all research utilizing a reservoir of systematic knowledge, including applied research, is designated as scientific research, then the relationship between science and technology appears as a much closer one. Even then it can be pointed out that many innovations are based on *ad hoc* knowledge or rule-of-thumb rather than on scientific principles. But then it can no longer be denied that many other innovations are related to a reservoir of systematic knowledge and are in fact, by definition, the outgrowth of science. On the basis of that second definition I would claim, then, that the development of much potentially harmful knowledge is not incidental but inherent in the very nature of scientific development itself.

In addition, it was argued earlier in the book, there are certain social arrangements that exacerbate and accelerate the harmful effects of science. In particular, they are those whereby pressure is being put on scientists to concentrate on practical problems and produce more and more practical results. For the more those practical results accumulate, the greater the probability that, if only by chance, some of them will be harmful. And in recent years pressures on scientists to produce practical results have been increasingly institutionalized. This is epitomized by the emergence and proliferation of the phenomenon of the Research and Development (R & D) laboratory, in both the private and government sectors. The growth of this phenomenon throughout this century and particularly in the postwar period has been spectacular and today there are thousands of R & D laboratories in the United States alone and a formidable part of all research is carried out in them (Layton, 1977).

The R & D laboratory is a complex research system which institutionally links research with practical goals. It integrates science into a corporate setting in which its contribution is constantly measured by its practical results. And since some of these practical results of science are necessarily harmful, these harmful effects have thus become a structural part of the scientific endeavour. Therefore they have come to be built into the socio-political role of the scientist who engages in this endeavour.

In the earlier part of this book it was also asserted that one thing was particularly worrying about this: namely, that the beneficial effects of the scientists' contributions have been petering out in recent years, whereas their deleterious effects, and the socio-political problems they have created, have become more prominent. In this chapter I shall present some concrete illustrations in support of these theses.

THE EFFECTS OF SCIENCE ON HEALTH AND LONGEVITY

The first illustration comes from the effects of science, and the scientists who create it, on physical health and on the length of human life. All throughout history, and up until very recently, the rates of human mortality were high, life-expectancy was short, and those surviving beyond the age of, say, 40 or 50 were few. Since the eighteenth century, however, we witness a steady decline of mortality and a consequent dramatic lengthening of life-expectancy. This development was due largely to a reduction of deaths from infectious diseases. It has customarily been thought that the decline of infectious disease was due largely to advances in medicine and particularly to medical measures of immunization and therapy.

Recently McKeown (1976) has convincingly made the case that, in fact, in the eighteenth and nineteenth centuries this decline was largely the result of improved nutrition and advances in hygiene and sanitation. From the second half of the nineteenth century onwards these included particularly purification of water, efficient disposal of sewage, provision of safe milk and improved personal and food hygiene (on this see also Mulkay, 1979a).

This goes to show that decline of mortality from infectious diseases was not as closely linked to developments in medicine, and particularly in personal medical treatment, as was previously thought. But it does not show that this decline in mortality was unrelated to scientific developments. Measures of water purification and improved hygiene with respect to milk, for instance, must surely have been influenced by science-derived knowledge on micro-organisms and their effects on human health.

Table 6.1   *Death Rates (per 1,000 Population) in Major Western Countries*

	1900	1950	1978/9
Austria	25·2	12·4	12·3
Belgium	19·3	12·0	11·7
Denmark	16·8	9·2	10·4
Finland	21·9	10·2	9·2
France	21·9	12·7	10·1
Germany	22·1	—	—
West Germany	—	10·5	11·6
Ireland	19·6	12·7	10·5
Italy	23·8	9·8	9·4
Netherlands	17·9	7·5	8·0
Norway	15·8	9·1	10·2
Sweden	16·8	10·0	11·0
Switzerland	19·3	10·1	9·2
United Kingdom:			
England and Wales	18·2	11·6	12·1
Scotland	18·5	12·5	12·7
United States	17·2	9·6	8·8

Sources: Mitchell, 1975, table B 6, pp. 117–24; United States Bureau of the Census, 1976, ser. B, 167–80, p. 59; World Health Organization, 1981, Vol. 4, pp. 12–16.

McKeown also shows that since the early twentieth century a closer link between the development of medicine and the decline in mortality has been forged. Thus the introduction in 1935 of sulphamides and later of antibiotics was an important (though not the only important) factor in the further decline of mortality in Western countries. This is noteworthy, because in the first half of the twentieth century, and even from 1935 onwards, mortality in Western countries continued to decline substantially while life-expectancy continued to rise (this is illustrated in Table 6.1 and Figures 6.1 and 6.2). There thus was a timespan, if only a short one perhaps, in which advances in medical science and advances in life-expectancy were visibly linked.

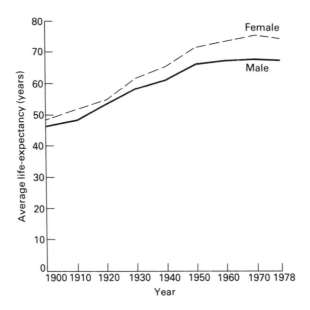

Figure 6.1   *Life-expectancy at birth in the United States.*
Sources: United States Bureau of the Census, 1976, ser. 107–15, p. 55; World Health Organization, 1981, Vol. 10, p. 431.

But as the table and figures show, from the middle of the twentieth century onwards mortality has been declining and life-expectancy has been rising only slightly. While the growth of longevity has thus levelled out, the problems created by science (i.e. scientists) for human health and hence for human life have become more prominent. For in recent years increasing evidence has accumulated to the effect that the drugs which scientists have created to cure disease have themselves induced new diseases and disabilities and, in many cases, have caused the death of the patients they were meant to heal. Of these, thalidomide, which has caused deformity in ten thousand babies, is the best known, but by no means the only example. As Silverman and Lee (1974, p. 261) see it: 'Although the magnitude of the problem remains unclear, there is ample evidence to show that it is serious.'

The risk of adverse effects from drugs is highest to hospitalized patients. As the same authors report, research by Schimmel (1964) found that among 1,000 patients admitted to an American hospital during an eight-month period, 1 per cent died of apparent drug reaction. Another study conducted in six American hospitals by Shapiro *et al.* (1971) indicated that the rate of fatal drug reactions in all medical patients was 0·44 per cent. 'If this figure were . . . applied to all patients admitted to all hospitals in the United States – a total of about 32 million admissions per year – it would indicate an annual total of more than 130,000 deaths' (Silverman and Lee, 1974, p. 264).

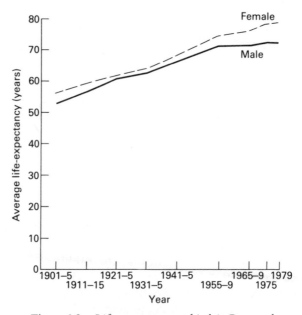

Figure 6.2   *Life-expectancy at birth in Denmark.*
Sources: United Nations, 1949, table 34, pp. 514–23; World Health Organization, 1981, Vol. 10, pp. 430–9.

The authors also estimate a total of more than 5 million serious adverse drug reactions a year among the population of the United States. When these numbers are projected to all modern Western countries where *mutandi mutandis* the situation is similar to that in the United States, the figures become even more staggering. More recently Melville and Johnson in their book *Cured to Death* (1983) report that in both the United States and Britain it has been calculated that more people die each year from prescribed drugs than by road accidents. They add (p. 6): 'There is no reason to believe that this level of casualties does not occur in every country where pharmaceutical products are widely used.'

To be sure, the number of people killed or suffering severe illness or incapacity through the intake of drugs in no way equals the number of people who have been cured by drugs. But this is small consolation to those who themselves, or whose close relatives, have become victims of such drugs. It seems, then, that by now the cure is, perhaps not worse than the disease, but distinctly suspect.

What is worse, the balance may soon be tipped in the opposite direction, as more and more drug-resistant micro-organisms and organisms develop. For instance, it has recently been reported that leprosy is spreading alarmingly in Third World countries, and is now affecting 12 million people worldwide. This is due to the increasing resistance of the disease-carrying micro-organisms to the drugs which have previously contained the disease.

Recently scientists have also had to admit that science is losing ground in the battle against disease-carrying mosquitoes. As Dr M. Dover, a researcher in the 'Global Pesticide Use Project' of the Washington-based World Resources Institute, and other scientists have noted, mosquitoes are developing multiple resistances and are becoming immune to almost every type of insecticide. Biological warfare against mosquitoes has not proved as effective as was previously hoped. As a result, some diseases carried by mosquitoes are rapidly rising around the world, including malaria and dengue fever. Drugs to treat and prevent malaria, such as chloroquine, are losing their effectiveness. There have been resurgences of deadly epidemics of malaria in parts of Asia, Africa and Central America, and there is a dengue epidemic now in some Central American countries and all over the Caribbean. The chances of introduction of the epidemics into the south-eastern United States are great (Broad, 1984).

Even closer to home a world expert, Professor Stuart Levy of the Tufts Medical School in Boston, has recently said (and thus has further publicized) what is becoming widely realized already: namely, that the widespread use of antibiotics has encouraged the growth of a variety of resistant strains of micro-organisms. This now seriously complicates the treatment of diseases which so far have been regarded as curable – including, for instance, meningitis, certain types of gonorrhoea, cholera, dysentery and typhoid. Frequently people get infected with such resistant strains of micro-organisms when already weakened by other diseases – in the Western world, particularly cancer. They then become untreatable. Mortality from cancer, one of the main killers in Western society, may thus partly disguise mortality from drug-resistant bacteria. Science has thus inadvertently helped develop more vigorous insects and micro-organisms whose contribution to mortality seems to be growing.

How and why did this situation arise? According to many knowledgeable observers, some of it is due to certain basic flaws in the manner in which medical drug-related research is carried out and in the manner in which the knowledge obtained in such research is disseminated. During the nineteenth and early twentieth centuries most new drugs were discovered by scientific investigators working privately. From the 1930s onwards, most of the research on the development of new drugs has been undertaken by scientists working in R & D laboratories in the pharmaceutical industry. Evidently the main motive for conducting such research is that of making a profit. As Silverman and Lee (1974, p. 24) observe:

Few if any other industries have contributed so magnificently to the health and welfare of the public, to the control of pain and sickness, and to the prolongation of life . . . At the same time, it has been able to capture financial rewards beyond the most optimistic dreams of its founders. If it exists secondarily for profits but primarily to benefit mankind, as some spokesmen have claimed, then the drug industry is much like the early missionaries who reportedly went to Hawaii to do good – and did exceedingly well.

The drug industry has defended its profits by the fact that there are many failures, for which successful drugs must compensate. On this, a former drug company research director commented: 'This is true since it is the very essence of research. The problem arises out of the fact that they market so many of their failures' (Silverman and Lee, 1974, p. 33).

In the United States the Food and Drug Administration (FDA) is in charge of monitoring pharmaceutical research and the licensing and advertising of drugs, as are government agencies (with various degrees of effectiveness) in other Western countries. Since 1938 a new drug cannot be put on the market until the manufacturer presents convincing proof to the FDA that it is relatively safe. Since 1962 adequate proof must also be supplied with regard to the effectiveness of the drug. The FDA now requires extensive research evidence of both before a new drug is allowed to go on the market, although in some other Western countries government requirements are less stringent.

However, much depends not only on how the research on drugs is conducted, but on how it is reported to the government agency and the physician, and on how the drugs are promoted. According to Selinger (1981), Silverman and Lee (1974) and many other observers, not only is it the case that the tests carried out on the possible harmful effects of new drugs have not always been adequate, but it is also the case that in reports on those tests adverse results are sometimes understated while beneficial effects are over-emphasized.

Despite the questionable validity of pharmaceutical manufacturers' advertising, medical practitioners obtain nearly all of their information on new drugs from those manufacturers. In America, for instance, the *Physicians' Desk Reference*, '. . . which is used by many physicians as the virtual bible of prescription drugs . . . is in fact simply a compilation of *paid advertising purchased by the major brand name companies*' (Silverman and Lee, 1974, p. 75). Similarly in Britain the *UK Monthly Index of Medical Specialities*, the most important prescribing guide for doctors, is compiled from details supplied by the indexed drug manufacturers (Medawar, 1979, pp. 115–21). In addition, as Silverman and Lee (1974, p. 50) report, 'Numerous surveys have shown repeatedly that many if not most medical men are first induced to prescribe a new product not by a scientific report in a medical journal but by a drug advertisement or, more often, by the presentation of a detail man.' All this causes not only faulty prescription but over-prescription as well for, as Selinger (1981, p. 204) points out, the drug companies are interested in teaching doctors to use drugs, but they are not interested 'in the equally important business of teaching doctors when not to use drugs'.

Ostensibly all these faulty procedures should have been held in check by the pharmaceutical manufacturers' drive for profit. These companies can be (and have been) sued and made to pay millions of dollars to those harmed by their products. But apparently the prospects of immediate profits outweigh the possible subsequent risks of required compensation payments in the future, payments which, in any case, never equal those profits.

However, the central point I would like to make is that all these faulty arrangements are only supplementary to the main cause of the situation: namely, the fact that a large part of modern medicine is based on drugs, and that no drug is absolutely safe. 'With few if any exceptions, any drug that will influence living tissues can also damage those tissues' (Silverman and Lee, 1974, p. 269). And, one may add, any drug that destroys harmful micro-organisms also helps breed resistant strains of micro-organisms whose destruction then becomes that much more difficult. And as scientific knowledge on drugs is increasing, medicine is relying on an increasing number of people being prescribed an increasing number of a dramatically growing variety of medications. Hence *as medical science is advancing, drugs are multiplying. And as drugs are multiplying and as their prescription and intake are proliferating, their harmful as well as their beneficial effects must necessarily multiply as well.* Proper research, promotion and prescription procedures could alleviate the problem but not eradicate it; they could slow down, but not prevent, its further growth.

Those who are usually blamed for this state of affairs are the pharmaceutical manufacturers, that is, the capitalists who are set to maximize profits and the government agencies who have not sufficiently clamped down on their faulty practices. This, however, is not the point of the present analysis. My concern here is to highlight the role of the intellectuals, the scientists, who conduct the research on new drugs for the pharmaceutical industry, and issue the pertinent research reports, and the role of the scientists in the government agencies who evaluate these reports. Because scientists have presented their endeavour as having practical utility, and because the pharmaceutical industry has perceived this practical utility as a source of profits, scientists in that industry are now under heavy pressure to develop drugs and produce positive research results appertaining to those drugs. Doubtless their careers and sometimes their very livelihood may depend on producing such results. As a consequence of the same developments scientists in government agencies in charge of licensing new drugs are evidently under heavy pressure from the pharmaceutical industry to speed up such licensing. Thus the institutional arrangements, partly constructed by scientists and now surrounding their role, open them to pressures. These, in turn, accelerate the process of realizing the harmful potential contained in medical science as such.

In sum, then, *the harmful effects of drugs now increasingly coming to the fore are not only the result of capitalist greed. They are the results of science. They are science. But they are exacerbated by social arrangements whereby the greed of the capitalist is now incorporated into the social role of the scientist.*

THE EFFECTS OF SCIENCE ON WARFARE

The same principles are best exemplified in another area, that of the role of today's scientists in the development of warfare. The alliance between Western science and armaments is by no means a new one. Almost from its very inception, and certainly from the seventeenth century onwards, Western science and scientists were heavily involved in the development of military technology. Thus Merton (1973, p. 208) has calculated that in four typical years in the seventeenth century, on average, about 10 per cent of the research carried out by the foremost scientific body in England, the Royal Society, was devoted to some aspect of military technology. The benefits which military technology derived from these experiments were considerable, and scientific involvement in this technology did not diminish in the eighteenth and nineteenth centuries.

In the twentieth century science's contribution to military technology has grown even further, as evidenced by the two world wars in which, courtesy of science and technology, tens of millions, including civilians, could be and were killed. In the First World War, for instance, the importance of science and technology for warfare became prominent especially with the development of poison gas. But advanced scientific and technical capabilities proved their value in many other sectors of the war effort as well, even though science was not yet decisive for the final outcome of the war (Schroeder-Gudehus, 1977).

The link between science and warfare was strengthened in the Second World War. Scientists not only worked on the development of weapons but also advised on their tactical deployment. The atomic bomb, of course, has been the weapon most closely identified with this development. But in terms of influencing the actual course of fighting, dozens of other developments such as radar, sonar and the proximity fuse were probably of equal importance. Taken together they undoubtedly had a decisive influence on the outcome of the war (Sapolsky, 1977).

But although the contribution of science to warfare is by no means new, and was escalating in the first half of the twentieth century, it is only in most recent years that this contribution has come to full fruition. For the potential mass killing ('mega-death') which military technology has conjured up since the Second World War is vastly greater than anything humanity has so far experienced. And it is precisely in the postwar era that the perfection of armaments has become a product of scientific research to an even greater extent than before. This holds true for nuclear, chemical and biological armaments (almost entirely a contribution of science to society) even more than it does for conventional ones.

Thus the scientist has given us a calculable extension of life-expectancy, which shows up impressively on statistical graphs. But the scientist has also detracted an incalculable quantity from that life-expectancy by giving us the means to destroy each other collectively. We will never know for sure how much of our life-expectancy has thereby been taken away. For if the unthinkable ever happens few, if any, will be left to plot the graphs and few, if any, will be left to look at them. But we do know something about the fear of nuclear war, the anxiety which has been created and which in recent years is apparently quite widespread, especially among youngsters in Western society (see, for instance, Blackwell and Gessner, 1983; Fiske *et al.*, 1983; Kramer *et al.*, 1983; Lipsey, 1980; Schwebel, 1982; and many others). In the words of J. Ben-David, 'Science . . . has replaced the all-pervading anxiety about illness with a new anxiety about the possibility of the total annihilation of mankind' (1971, p. 182).

As a consequence of the scientists' contribution we are now in a situation in which the capability to destroy all of us is gradually being acquired not only by ever larger numbers, but also by ever less reliable social bodies. The first stage, past already, was one in which only the super powers had that capability. At that stage people could still lull themselves into comfort with the notion that these powers are ruled by relatively rational groups of people. The next stage, which we are witnessing now, is one where the capability to destroy us is rapidly extending to a large number of smaller countries.[1] The chances of it eventually falling into the hands of hard-pressed or threatened countries or into the hands of mentally unstable rulers is commensurately increasing.

The third stage, which we have not reached yet but which is a logical sequel to the two previous ones, is that of nuclear globally destructive weapons falling into the hands of non-governmental, terrorist, or other unaccountable types of people or organizations. This becomes evident, for instance, in the following excerpt from a report entitled *Technological Change and Employment* (1983, p. 119) issued by the Australian Department of Science and Technology:

A new kind of terrorism using sophisticated technology is

possible, especially in the field of nuclear technology. The chairman of the UK Atomic Energy Agency, Sir John Hill, acknowledged that there are literally dozens of books, periodicals, and unclassified publications available which contain information on the construction of nuclear weapons and nuclear parts. In 1972, a leaflet appeared in London entitled 'Towards a People's Bomb' which purported to describe how plutonium could be extracted and a crude nuclear weapon made by agencies other than governments. The claim was viewed with the greatest scepticism, but since then there have been confirmations from many other sources of the availability outside governments of the know-how for the construction of a crude nuclear device. With information publicly available, students have been known to put together workable blueprints for such a device, the best known instance being the effort of an MIT undergraduate commissioned for this purpose by a television company ... The most recent information on terrorist organisations is not only that they operate world-wide, but that they often have links with each other exchanging information and arms. In this context a weakly guarded convoy of nuclear waste being moved out for disposal is an invitation for terrorists.

That the threat of nuclear terrorism is a real one is suggested by the fact that it has prompted the United States government to create a special organization to combat it. Called the Nuclear Emergency Search Team (or NEST), it can call on 250 atomic physicists, weapon designers, bomb disposal experts and others to assist in its operations. Its procedures and plans for action have already been set out. But whether, if the occasion ever arises, it will be successful in its operations no one can foretell. Besides, dangers of nuclear terrorism exist in other countries as well, and they proliferate along with the proliferation of nuclear weapons.

No less worrying is the possibility of massive nuclear war resulting from an accident. At least two near-accidents of this sort have occurred already. The first one was the result of the following episode, recently recounted by former United States Defense Secretary Robert McNamara.[2] In 1961, during the

Kennedy administration, a US bomber carrying nuclear weapons crashed and one of the bombs was nearly detonated. 'The bomb's arming mechanism had six or seven manoeuvres to go through to detonate, but the bomber crashed and the arming mechanism went through six of the seven,' he said. He seemed to imply that an accidental nuclear explosion in North Carolina might have been misconstrued as a Soviet strike, and triggered a full-fledged nuclear war.

The story was subsequently corroborated by two former Pentagon officials who said that a B52 bomber had indeed jettisoned two 24-megaton bombs before it crashed. One bomb had broken apart on impact, contaminating the area with plutonium. A parachute on the second bomb and only a single safety switch prevented an explosion 1,800 times more powerful than the Hiroshima bomb in 1945.

The second near-accident occurred in 1979, when a computer error had the United States Defense Department notified of an imminent Soviet nuclear attack. According to some claims, the United States was three minutes away from pressing the button.[3] Whatever it was that averted the disaster, we may not be quite as lucky the next time around.

Ostensibly the 'hot line' between the American president and the Soviet leader is designed to forestall accidents of this sort. It is difficult, however, to see how it could be effective. Imagine a case where the United States Defense Department's computers show an imminent Soviet nuclear attack on the United States. The president is alerted and contacts the Soviet leader asking him if he has launched an attack. If he has not, and the whole thing is a computer error, his reply will obviously be 'No'. But if he has launched an attack, it is in his country's interest to keep the American president from knowing the truth for as long as possible. Hence his reply in this case, too, will be 'No'. The president knows this, of course, and therefore cannot place too much reliance on the Soviet reply. At a certain point, when the signals of approaching missiles become sufficiently clear, he must, hot line or no hot line, give the order to press the button. And the same would be true for a reverse occurrence. The effectiveness of the hot line in preventing an accidental nuclear war thus depends basically on mutual trust. But if there were such trust, then nuclear armaments would be superfluous to begin with.

A no lesser (though less publicized) science-created danger is that of biological and particularly of chemical weaponry, as can be gleaned once more from the above-mentioned report on technological change published by the Australian Department of Science and Technology (1983, pp. 154–5):

> Since 1975 there has been a resurgence of activity in chemical warfare preparations in the US and presumably also in the USSR. US chemical war research expenditure has mounted from $29 million in 1976 to $106 million in 1981 ... Appalling effects of chemical warfare were seen during World War I, when hydrogen cyanide and mustard gas were among the weapons which caused 1,300,000 casualties, including 90,000 deaths and 100,000 permanent disabilities. The signatories of the 1925 Geneva Protocol pledged not to be the first users of chemical weapons in future wars but their use in retaliation is therefore not ruled out. Unlike biological weapons (germ warfare), the use of which was completely renounced by the US in 1969, chemical weapons remain a very live part of its arsenal: the US is estimated to have 37,000 tonnes of mustard gas and about 130,000 tonnes of nerve gas which, with other chemicals, total about 400,000 tonnes ... The coresponding Soviet figures are not known ... The production of vast quantities of similar chemicals in industry is continuously in progress.

The danger of terrorists acquiring and using chemical or biological weapons is even greater than the risk of them acquiring nuclear devices. According to an authoritative report by the Institute for Foreign Policy Analysis recently published in Washington, the most deadly chemical weapons, nerve gases, are as easy to manufacture as insecticides. Anyone with a master's degree in biochemistry could manufacture them using a laundry room or garage. Anyone without such a degree could easily steal them from one of the countless research laboratories in the United States and overseas, *and some are even available by mail order in the USA.*

Fifty-five terrorist groups potentially capable of using chemical/biological (C/B) weapons have been listed in the United States alone. They have not been used so far, according to the study, because the ends of terrorism have been achieved easily enough by explosives and other conventional means. However, as the use of bombs and bullets becomes increasingly common, terrorists' competition for publicity may well encourage an escalation into C/B weapons. Already various groups have flirted with C/B. The Symbionese Liberation Army, active in California in the early 1970s, dipped its bullets in poison and was found to have manuals on biological warfare in its possession. In 1974 a demented Los Angeles engineer actually manufactured nerve agents and threatened the then president, Richard Nixon, in a tape-recording sent to the White House (Samuel, 1984).

One worrying possibility is that terrorists may obtain radioactive material and threaten to contaminate an area or drop it into a city's water supply. The same danger, of course, looms with regard to other chemical weapons. Biological weapons in particular are uniquely adaptive to sabotage; small amounts of material, strategically placed, could cause extensive casualties.

Prestigious institutions such as the Swedish Institute of Peace Research have issued warnings, on the basis of certain calculations, that a nuclear (chemical or biological) catastrophe within the next decade is nearly a certainty unless there are drastic changes in public attitudes and government actions (Weeramantry, 1983, p. 121). Others have used probability theory to calculate that any event which has an undiminishing probability of occurring (even if such a probability be of a small magnitude) will eventually occur. Whether or not the probability of the occurrence of such a disaster can be calculated, such an occurrence is in any case a very real possibility.

How can the fact that we now find ourselves in this situation be explained? And who is to take the blame for it? The first point to remind ourselves of is that the evolving scientific (e.g. nuclear physics) knowledge which goes into the production of advanced weaponry is the self-same one that is also being utilized for peaceful purposes. The utilization of science for peaceful usage and its utilization for warfare are thus but two sides of the same coin; both are inherent in the development of science itself. And the more science develops, the more it serves as a basis for both types of application.

Some commentators have gone as far as to suggest that once usable scientific knowledge exists it necessarily *will* be used for military no less than for peaceful purposes (see Ellul, 1965; Lapp, 1970; Yanarella, 1975). Sapolsky (1977) has convincingly rebutted this by showing that feasible weapon developments are not infrequently cancelled by governments. But while not all applicable knowledge is necessarily applied, it is but a tautology to point out that all such knowledge *can* be applied. And the more knowledge develops, the *greater the chances* that some of it will be applied for military no less than for peaceful purposes.

While the increasing dangers emanating from scientific knowledge are thus inherent in science itself, they have also been exacerbated by social arrangements; scientific knowledge applicable to warfare has become more widely available and the chances of it actually being applied have grown commensurately. Another social factor has been the increasing pressure being put on scientists in these areas to produce more and more practical results. Some observers have pointed out that, as in the drug industry, these pressures result from the profit motive of capitalists. The participation of profit-making organizations in the weapons production process provides an obvious financial incentive for the continuous development of new weapons. Others have stressed the importance of the military establishment in pressing for an accelerated rate of weapon development (see, for example, Greenwood, 1975; Head, 1973; Sapolsky, 1977).

It seems, however, that here another and perhaps more important social factor is at work. For this 'Project Manhattan', for the production of the first atomic bomb, furnishes an obvious example. As will be recalled, the first atomic bomb was developed in the United States during the Second World War to avert the threat that Nazi Germany would be the first to have the bomb and use it. Albert Einstein, who during some parts of his life was a committed pacifist, nevertheless gave the development of the bomb his blessing on those grounds. The scientists and engineers who participated in 'Project Manhattan', the actual construction of the bomb, had similar motives.

Had it not been for Nazi Germany, similar misgivings with regard to the Soviet Union would probably have prompted Western scientists to similar action. And had Western scientists not developed the bomb, it would probably still have been brought into being by Soviet scientists and engineers worried at being overtaken by the West. And had Soviet scientists not developed atomic weapons, scientists in other countries with similar misgivings would eventually have provided the knowledge necessary for their development. This, in turn, is the reason why Western scientists and engineers developed them in the first place.

The scientists involved in the production of the atomic bomb were thus under enormous pressure to do so, and this pressure emanated from the fear that scientists in other countries would precede them and pre-empt their discoveries. Those scientists, in turn, laboured under similar fears, so that a vicious circle developed whereby their fears were mutually validating. The same situation persists today, as the fear of being overtaken by others acts as a powerful source of pressure on scientists. It also acts as a source of legitimation for the scientific-military endeavour of perfecting ever more destructive mega-weapons, the source of which, however, lies in the growth of science itself.

What all this amounts to is that the development of science now includes the provision of constantly advancing knowledge on the perfection of mega-weapons. *The development of that knowledge is the result, not of a deliberate decision on the part of this or the other group of scientists, but of the very dynamics of science itself.* Socio-political pressures brought to bear on scientists have certainly speeded up the process, but the absence of such pressures could not have prevented it.

THE EFFECTS OF SCIENCE ON LIVING STANDARDS

Nowhere is the two-sided effect of science and scientists more evident than in their contribution to economic production and through it to our standard of life, and nowhere can the above-presented theses be better supported by concrete illustrations than in this area.

Modern society owes the unprecedented rise in the standard of living which has been evident since the second half of the nineteenth century and up until recent years, at least in part to the application of science to the process of production.[4] As is widely recognized, it is the recently strengthened link of scientific (albeit frequently applied) research with industry that has brought about the constant accelerating technological innovations leading to the vast increases in productivity which, in turn, have made a major contribution to our soaring levels of consumption. But technological development has also contributed to the creation of unemployment, and thus to the depression of living standards for a significant proportion of the population.

It has done so almost since its inception, and Marx in his time was already aware of this when he wrote: 'Machinery . . . [is] replacing skilled workers by unskilled . . . throwing the hand workers on to the streets in masses, and, where it is developed, improved and replaced by more productive machinery . . . discharging workers in smaller batches' ([1849] 1977, p. 266).

At that time, and for many years to come, advancing technology, while making some jobs redundant, created new ones to take their place. Of this, too, Marx was aware as he wrote 'The economists tell us . . . that the workers rendered superfluous by machinery find new branches of employment', although he added 'They dare not assert directly that the same workers who are discharged, find places in the new branches of labour. The facts cry out too loudly against this lie' (ibid.).

For a long time, then, advancing industrial technology has created unemployment and its accompanying misery for some people but employment for others. Further, throughout a large part of the nineteenth century advancing industrial technology was the creation of talented inventors who were indifferent to science. Scientists, therefore, could hardly be held responsible for either the positive or the negative results of these advances.

Since then, however, two developments have occurred. First, according to many observers, industry is now based on a closer link between science and technology. As B. Aptheker (1972, p. 53), for instance, has noted, it is especially since the Second World War that scientific research has become a prerequisite for technological change. Secondly, advancing technology has gone one step further in the creation of unemployment; it is still abolishing jobs for some people and creating them for others, but through micro-electronics and computerization it is apparently making more jobs redundant than it is creating.

Present-day technological change may be differentiated into two types: product and process change. The former refers to the development of knowledge serving as basis for the introduction of new, frequently more rational and efficient, products; the latter involves development of knowledge aimed at rationalizing the production of existing ones. The former usually leads to increased levels of production in an industry or to the creation of new industries (for instance, those associated with micro-ovens or food processors) and therefore to the creation of new jobs. The latter, in contrast, though also leading to increased production is often designed to displace labour (for instance, through the introduction of robots in manufacturing industries). Recent technological change, though generally increasing production, thus both creates employment and displaces labour. However, in recent years the latter effect has become the more prominent.

This is attested to by the report of the Australian Department of Science and Technology (1983) cited earlier in another context. It is also attested to by the Reagan administration's recent estimates, according to which 6·5 per cent of the American workforce is 'structurally' unemployed, that is, is unemployed because of technological development; and this percentage may climb even higher in the future (Kilborn, 1983). The situation in other Western countries is not likely to be much different.

The causes for this situation are well exemplified by the following account by Weeramantry (1983, p. 118) who writes that an average clerk works a total of 80,000 hours in a lifetime, adding that in some cases 'the clerical contribution of such a person throughout his or her working life can be matched by a computer in four minutes'.

As was noted in previous chapters, the present high rates of unemployment all over the Western world have come into being following the economic recession of the last decade. Even so, it is clear from the preceding discussion, and widely accepted today, that a large part of unemployment is brought about by long-term technological change rather than by short-term fluctuations in the economy. The main point I would like to stress, however, is not merely that science today is at the basis of advancing technology which creates unemployment. It is not even merely that science today is at the root both of our generally high living standard and of our higher levels of unemployment from which a lower living standard for some and much human misery emanates. It is rather that *the same facets of science have this two-pronged effect. The knowledge employed in the rationalization and increase of production, the process that has created our higher standard of living, is also the very one that now creates our higher levels of unemployment.* The latter is *thus not a by-product but inherent in the very essence of the evolving effects of science on society.*

It may be argued that scientists, together with computer experts, engineers, and other intermediaries, by providing the basis for automation, have merely created the potential for more effective production. It is now up to the economists, and those who base policies on their advice, to devise the strategies that will utilize this potential entirely for the benefit, rather than the detriment, of society. It may further be argued that by creating the potential for more effective production scientists have also presented society with an increased potential for leisure. It is now up to the sociologists, and those who base policies on their advice, to work out how this leisure is to be distributed and how it is to be utilized creatively.

Alternatively it may be argued that it is up to the social scientists to work out how the jobs made redundant in production are to be replaced by jobs in the tertiary sector, in areas such as teaching, health care and the like, once more for the greater welfare of society. It is thus up to the social scientists to work out how increased unemployment, or increased leisure, is to be prevented from creating an 'underclass' of outcasts who no longer share in the affluence of modern society (see

Chapter 4). But this merely passes the buck from one faction of the Knowledge Elite to another. And this other group of intellectuals might well be excused if it were inclined to pass the buck back again with the assertion that the scientists ought to be the ones to solve the problem they themselves have, directly or indirectly, brought into being. Perhaps the fairest conclusion would be that various parts of the Knowledge Elite might share responsibility for the problem.

My concern in this chapter, however, is not with apportioning the blame among various groups of intellectuals, but rather with the role that exact science and the scientists who work within its disciplines have been playing in the creation of unemployment; and here one cannot escape the conclusion that this role has been considerable and has become more prominent in recent years.

CONCLUSION

For the last few centuries science, in particular Western science, has spelt 'progress', and in many ways it continues to do so. The scientists who have created and developed it have thus made many outstanding contributions to the welfare of modern society. At the same time, it is clear by now that through their scientific endeavour scientists have presented society with a series of socio-political problems, some of which have been briefly reviewed in this chapter.

While the post-industrialists have argued that the impact of science (and scientists) on society is basically salubrious and that any negative effects it may have are incidental, I have in this chapter illustrated the point that the negative no less than the positive effects of science (and scientists) on society are inherent in the very development of science itself and therefore are practically inevitable and not easily eliminated. At the same time, I have shown that these negative effects have been exacerbated by certain social processes and that these too have become largely irreversible today.

While the post-industrialists have asserted that the contribution which scientific knowledge has recently made to society's welfare is greater than ever before, I have shown in this chapter that the reverse is the truth; the contribution that science has made to the welfare of society, as distinct from the development of science itself, has recently passed its peak and, conversely, the problems it has created have loomed larger. The question that logically follows from this discussion is whether the scientist in his or her socio-political role does not now carry moral responsibility for an endeavour whose balance sheet for society is increasingly on the negative rather than the positive side.

And yet it is precisely when science's contribution to society is becoming so questionable that scientists must increasingly legitimize their endeavour by this contribution and draw their livelihood from it. With the co-operation of scientists, science has increasingly become corporate science, research and development have become inextricably linked with each other, and both have become increasingly linked with profit and with the political goals of governments. Hence the pressures for practical results and the dangers of these results have concomitantly increased. The increasing pressures on scientists to produce practical results and the increasing dangers of such results are thus two trends which have recently converged in the role of the Western scientist.

NOTES: CHAPTER 6

1   According to a new report from the United Nations Association in the United States, six countries now have nuclear weapons; another ten countries are believed capable of building such weapons or are doing so already; another eleven could have them within six years if they wished.
2   Reported in the *Canberra Times*, 16 September 1983.
3   Reported in the *Weekend Australian*, 16–17 July 1983.
4   Modern economic development has evidently been brought about by a combination of factors; the literature analysing these is enormous and this is not the place to go into its intricacies. (For a brief review of some of this literature, see Etzioni-Halevy, 1981.) Analysts agree, however, that science and its application to production have played a major part in this combination of factors.

Conclusion

This is a book on the Knowledge Elite, that is to say, on intellectuals; it is for intellectuals, by an intellectual, but it is not designed to please intellectuals. It is basically a demystification of the socio-political role many intellectuals have purported to play in modern Western society; it is an attempt to debunk their role as self-proclaimed prophets, in charge of foretelling things to come and in charge of guiding society towards a better future devised by themselves. Its main thesis has been that intellectuals are prophets who have failed because there is an inherent disparity between the knowledge they have to offer and its usefulness for society; because many of their forecasts of the future on the basis of that knowledge have been wide of the mark; and because the guidance many of them have purported to offer society on the basis of that knowledge recently has not brought about the good things they promised it would, and has even helped exacerbate the problems now faced by Western society. Yet, like the failed prophets described by Festinger and his associates in 1956, members of the Knowledge Elite have nevertheless continued to legitimize their intellectual endeavour in terms of its supposed usefulness for society and they have continued to do so more adamantly than ever since it has become increasingly clear that this usefulness is questionable at best.

In the last part of the book this thesis was illustrated with respect to economists and some natural and physical scientists because those are the sections of the Knowledge Elite which have been most highly revered by policy-makers and the rest of the community. But other illustrations could have been given with equal validity. For instance, about sociologists (the intellectuals of my own discipline) it has been written that they dive the deepest and come out the muddiest. Certainly much could be said in support of this view whenever sociology is invoked for the guidance of social policy. Perhaps the only reason it would be difficult to make a generalization in this respect is because there are as many sociologies as there are sociologists – a fact which muddles the policy terrain even further. And intellectuals of many other disciplines are not exempt from the same criticism, either.

Although this may sound like a summary indictment of intellectuals, it is not meant to be. I have no quarrel with intellectuals when, as private citizens, they work for the improvement of society. I do not dispute that intellectuals, like all citizens in a democracy, have the right, some would say the duty, to be politically and socially active in order to bring about a better future. The problem arises only when intellectuals attempt to wed their intellectual endeavour to their socio-political activity, when they try to weld them together and make them appear as one. The problem arises, in other words, only when intellectuals enter the domain of policy and politics *qua intellectuals*, when they presume to have special qualifications for this purpose, when they purport to contribute to policy under the cloak of academic competence, diplomas and titles. The problem arises when members of the Knowledge Elite do little to dispel, and even encourage, the popular misconception that they are qualified to solve problems which, in fact, they do not know how to confront. The problem arises when members of the Knowledge Elite collaborate in the construction of their own social role in such a way that they are under mounting pressure to produce knowledge with practical results. It arises when these results are presented as beneficial, whereas in fact they are becoming increasingly fraught with risks and dangers for individuals and society.

I have said that this book is not designed to please intellectuals. This is so not only, or even chiefly, because it does little to bolster the intellectuals' collective ego, or because it presents a critique of their socio-political roles. For, after all, intellectuals are constantly criticizing each other; criticism is part and parcel of the intellectual endeavour and intellectuals normally thrive on mutual critiques. Rather, this book is unlikely to be pleasing to intellectuals because it criticizes (something intellectuals are fond of doing) but offers no advice (something intellectuals are even fonder of doing).

In a book entitled *What Is To Be Done?*, V. I. Lenin

purported to offer a solution to capitalist exploitation through revolution and detailed the practical guidelines for that revolution. Some decades later, in a book entitled *What Is To Be Undone?* (1974), M. Albert presented a critique of these and similar guidelines and ideologies and of what they had done, and raised the question of what needed to be undone to repair the damage. In a similar vein, this book presents no guidelines for what is to be done but rather raises the question of what is to be undone. In particular, it raises the question of whether perhaps the knot between the intellectual and the practical endeavour needs to be undone or loosened.

But the book does not purport to furnish an answer to this question. It thus purports to offer solutions neither to the problems of Western society nor to the problems of intellectuals who have entangled themselves in trying to offer such solutions, unsuccessfully. In fact, had I tried to offer solutions or guidelines to solutions for either set of problems, I would be doing precisely what I have argued intellectuals are not qualified to do; I would be perpetrating the very error I criticize in others. Had I purported to offer solutions to either the problems of society or the problems of intellectuals in advising society, I would be presenting the very type of prophecy which I claim has so conspicuously failed. To be sure, the book may then be criticized for having no practical relevance. But the point I am trying to make in this book is precisely that the intellectual endeavour contains its own justification and *does not require the legitimation of practical utility.*

It must be admitted that intellectuals in Western society face a dilemma. If they concentrate solely on the creation of knowledge they will be accused of secluding themselves in an ivory tower, of being socially unconcerned and irrelevant. If they step out into the world and dispense practical advice they will be accused, as they are in the present book, of detracting from, perhaps more than they are contributing to, the welfare of Western society. Intellectuals are thus in a no-win situation; their role is open to criticism either way.

But is this the type of problem that actually has a solution? And do the problems facing Western society today – the problems to which intellectuals have unsuccessfully attempted to supply remedies – in fact have solutions? To my mind, both are moot questions.

Western society has often been characterized as having a singularly active approach to nature and society, to life in general. And indeed there seems to be an implicit but widely held notion that 'where there is a will there is a way'; where there is a problem there must also be a solution, if only one works hard enough to find it. Certainly intellectuals have been among the front runners in promoting this approach, as they have purported to offer solutions to every conceivable human problem. Indeed, the prevalence of this approach among Western intellectuals may well have contributed to the unprecedented scientific, technological and economic development of Western society. But in recent years this approach seems to have become more and more questionable as the intellectuals' attempts to solve existing problems have increasingly contributed to the creation of more prominent and increasingly intractable problems. By the same token, I would argue, such an hyperactive approach to the intellectuals' own problems would be but another exercise in futility.

What, then, is the conclusion of all this? By now it should be clear that this book has no conclusion, at least no practical conclusion. Its aim has not been to provide answers but to raise questions, not to furnish solutions but to raise awareness of problems. This is not a 'how to . . .' book but a polemic. It is a critique of the role of intellectuals whose central aim is to provoke counter-critique and controversy amongst intellectuals. If this happens on even a small scale this book will have achieved its goal.

At the end, as an epilogue, I should like to return to the beginning. In the book of Genesis it is recounted that human beings were originally forbidden to acquire knowledge. Adam and Eve contravened this prescription when they ate the fruit of the tree of knowledge; in a way, they thus became the first intellectuals. In retribution for this primeval sin God decreed that humanity would be destined to die and to return to dust. At no time has this ancient legend made more sense than at the present time, when some types of knowledge are indeed becoming more and more dangerous and are beginning to jeopardize the very existence of humanity. From the vantage point of present-day civilization it would thus be apt to conclude with an expression of hope: that when the Almighty decreed that the acquisition of knowledge would lead humanity to return to dust – He did not mean it too literally.

References

Abercombie, N., and Urry, J. (1983), *Capital, Labour and the Middle Classes* (London: Allen & Unwin).

Ahluwalia, M. S. (1974), 'Income inequalities', in H. Chenery, M. S. Ahluwalia, C. L. G. Bell, J. H. Duloy and R. Jolly, *Redistribution with Growth* (London: Oxford University Press), pp. 3–37.

Albert, M. (1974), *What Is To Be Undone?* (Boston, Mass.: Porter Sargent).

Anderson, D. S. (1983), 'The use of social science knowledge in policy formation', Work in Progress seminar, Department of Sociology, Research School of Social Sciences, The Australian National University, 20 October.

Anderson, D. S., and Biddle, B. J. (1982), 'Social research, policy and educational practice', working papers in Sociology, Research School of Social Sciences, The Australian National University.

Aptheker, B. (1972), *The Academic Rebellion in the United States* (Secaucus, NJ: Citadel Press).

Aron, R. (1967), *The Industrial Society* (New York: Praeger).

Australian Department of Science and Technology (1983), *Technological Change and Employment* (Canberra: Australian Government Publishing Service).

Australian Electoral Office (1983a), *Research Report: A Quantitative Assessment of Electoral Enrolment in Australia* (Canberra: Australian Government Publishing Service).

Australian Electoral Office (1983b), *Research Report: A Qualitative Analysis of Attitudes Towards Enrolment and Voting* (Canberra: Australian Government Publishing Service).

Australian Financial Review (1983), 30 December.

Australian, The (1983), 27 July.

Bagwell, P. S., and Mingay, G. E. (1970), *Britain and America 1850–1939* (London: Routledge & Kegan Paul).

Barker, G. (1982), 'The poverty of economics', *The Age*, 20 November, p. 11.

Bell, D. (1973), *The Coming of the Post Industrial Society* (New York: Basic Books).

Bell, D. (1975), 'The revolution of rising entitlements', *Fortune*, April, pp. 98–103.

Ben-David, J. (1971), *The Scientist's Role in Society* (Englewood Cliffs, NJ: Prentice-Hall).

Berthoud, R. (1976), *The Disadvantages of Inequality* (London: Macdonald & Jane's).

Blackwell, P., and Gessner, J. C. (1983), 'Fear and trembling – an inquiry into adolescent perceptions of living in the nuclear age', *Youth and Society*, vol. 15, pp. 238–55.

Böhme, G. (1977), 'Models for the development of science', in Spiegel-Rösing and de Solla Price (eds), op. cit., pp. 319–51.

Bottomore, T. B. (1964), *Elites and Society* (London: Watts).

Boulding, K. E. (1964), *The Meaning of the Twentieth Century* (New York: Harper & Row).

Bowden, R. (1983), 'Stone shoots down a Keynesian', *The Australian*, 5 July, p. 1.

British Academy (1961), *Research in the Humanities and Social Sciences* (London: Oxford University Press).

Broad, W. (1984), 'The ancient mosquito has become a genetic menace', *The Age*, 25 July, p. 10.

Broom, L., and Jones, F. L. (with the collaboration of Zubrzycki, J.) (1976), *Opportunity and Attainment in Australia* (Canberra: Australian National University Press).

Broom, L., and Selznick, P. (1977), *Sociology* (New York: Harper & Row, 6th edn).

Brown, B. E. (1980), *Intellectuals and Other Traitors* (New York: Ark House).

Bruce-Briggs, B. (ed.) (1979), *The New Class* (New Brunswick, NJ: Transaction Books).

Brym, R. J. (1980), *Intellectuals and Politics* (London: Allen & Unwin).

Brzezinski, Z. (1970), *Between Two Ages* (New York: Viking Press).

Bulletin, The (1983), 5 April, pp. 20–5.

Canberra Times, The (1983), 16 September, p. 4.

Caplan, N., Morrison, A., and Stambaugh, R. J. (1975), *The Use of Social Science Knowledge in Policy Decisions at the National Level* (Ann Arbor, Mich.: Institute for Social Research).

Cherns, A. (1979), *Using the Social Sciences* (London: Routledge & Kegan Paul).

Chirot, D. (1977), *Social Change in the Twentieth Century* (New York: Harcourt Brace Jovanovich).

Clark, D. (1983a), 'After the Summit', *The Australian Financial Review*, 17 May, pp. 12–13.

Clark, D. (1983b), 'Keynes: the last polymath', *The Australian Financial Review*, 10 June, p. 35.

Crozier, M., Huntington, S. P., and Watanuki, J. (1975), *The Crisis of Democracy* (New York: New York University Press).

Dahrendorf, R. (1959), *Class and Class Conflict in Industrial Society* (Stanford, Calif.: Stanford University Press).

Draper, T. (1977), 'Intellectuals in politics', *Encounter*, vol. 49, pp. 47–60.

Drucker, P. (1971), *The Age of Discontinuity* (London: Heinemann).

Dye, T. R., and Zeigler, L. H. (1975), *The Irony of Democracy* (North Scituate, Mass.: Duxbury Press).

Economist, The (1983), 14 May, 10 September.

Eisenstadt, S. N. (1966), *Modernization: Protest and Change* (Englewood Cliffs, NJ: Prentice-Hall).

126   *The Knowledge Elite and the Failure of Prophecy*

Ellul, J. (1965), *The Technological Society* (New York: Vintage Books).

Etzioni-Halevy, E. (1981), *Social Change* (London: Routledge & Kegan Paul).

Etzioni-Halevy, E. (1983a), *Bureaucracy and Democracy* (London: Routledge & Kegan Paul).

Etzioni-Halevy, E. (1983b), 'Has the New Right curbed the growth of bureaucracy?', paper presented to the Annual American Sociological Association Conference, Detroit, August.

Festinger, L., Riecken, H. W., and Schachter, S. (1956), *When Prophecy Fails* (Minneapolis, Minn.: University of Minnesota Press).

Feyerabend, P. (1975), *Against Method* (London: New Left Books).

Field, G. L., and Higley, J. (1982), 'The population surplus', *Times Higher Education Supplement*, 15 October, pp. 13–14.

Fiske, S. T., Pratto, F., and Pavelchak, M. A. (1983), 'Citizens' images of nuclear war', *Journal of Social Issues*, vol. 39, pp. 41–65.

Frank, A. G. (1971), *Sociology of Development and Underdevelopment of Sociology* (London: Pluto Press).

Friedman, M. (1983), 'The Keynesian legacy', *The Weekend Australian Magazine*, 18–19 June.

Galbraith, J. K. (1967), *The New Industrial State* (Boston, Mass.: Houghton Mifflin).

Gans, H. J. (1973), *More Equality* (New York: Pantheon).

Gibbons, M., and Johnson, C. (1970), 'Relationship between science and technology', *Nature*, no. 2227, 11 July, p. 125.

Gibson, Q. B. (1973), 'The growth of knowledge', unpublished.

Gouldner, A. W. (1979), *The Future of Intellectuals and the Rise of the New Class* (London: Macmillan).

Great Britain Central Statistical Office (1983), *Social Trends*, no. 13 (London: HMSO).

Greenwood, T. (1975), *Making the MIRV* (Cambridge, Mass.: Ballinger).

Haines, J. (1977), *The Politics of Power* (London: Cape).

Halsey, A. H. (1983), 'Growing up unequal', *Times Educational Supplement*, 16 September, p. 4.

Hardin, C. L., and Rosenberg, A. (1982), 'In defense of convergent realism', *Philosophy of Science*, vol. 49, pp. 604–15.

Hausman, D. M. (1981), 'Are general equilibrium theories explanatory?', in J. C. Pitt (ed.), *Philosophy in Economics* (London: Reidel), pp. 17–32.

Head, R. G. (1973), 'Doctrinal innovation and the A-7 attack aircraft decisions', in R. G. Head and E. J. Rokke (eds), *American Defense Policy* (Baltimore, Md.: Johns Hopkins University Press, 3rd edn), pp. 431–45.

Heyworth Committee (1965), *Report of the Committee on Social Studies* (London: HMSO).

Horowitz, I. L. (ed.) (1971), *The Use and Abuse of Social Science* (New Brunswick, NJ: Transaction Books).

Huhne, C. (1983), 'Oxford experts declare guru Friedman raked', *The Age*, 19 December, p. 18.

Huntington, S. P. (1968), *Political Order in Changing Societies* (New Haven, Conn.: Yale University Press).

Kahn, H. (1962), *Thinking about the Unthinkable* (London: Weidenfeld & Nicolson).

Katz, H. S. (1976), *The Paper Aristocracy* (New York: Books in Focus).

Keynes, J. M. (1971), *A Tract on Monetary Reform*, Vol. IV in *The Collected Writings of John Maynard Keynes* (London: Macmillan/St Martin's Press, 2nd edn).

Kilborn, P. T. (1983), 'Recession's deep bit marks expected to remain', *Australian Financial Review*, 6 June, p. 7.

Kincaid, J. C. (1973), *Poverty and Equality in Britain* (Harmondsworth: Penguin).

King, A. (1975), 'Overload', *Political Studies*, vol. 23, pp. 284–96.

Knorr, K. D. (1977), 'Policymakers' use of social science knowledge', in Weiss (ed.), op. cit., pp. 165–82.

Konrád, G., and Szelényi, I. (1979), *The Intellectuals on the Road to Class Power*, trans. A. Arato and R. E. Allen (Brighton: Harvester).

Kramer, B. M., Kalick, S. M., and Milborn, M. A. (1983), 'Attitudes toward nuclear weapons and nuclear war: 1945–1982', *Journal of Social Issues*, vol. 39, pp. 7–24.

Kumar, K. (1978), *Prophecy and Progress* (London: Allen Lane).

Lakatos, I. (1972), 'Falsification and the methodology of scientific research programs', in I. Lakatos and A. Musgrave (eds), *Criticism and the Growth of Knowledge* (New York and London: Cambridge University Press, 2nd edn), pp. 91–195.

Lapp, R. (1970), *Arms Beyond Doubt* (New York: Cowles).

Laudan, L. (1977), *Progress and its Problems* (London: Routledge & Kegan Paul).

Laudan, L. (1979), 'Historical methodologies', in P. D. Asquith and H. E. Kyburg (eds), *Current Research in Philosophy of Science* (East Lansing, Mich.: Philosophy of Science Association), pp. 40–54.

Laudan, L. (1981), 'A confutation of convergent realism', *Philosophy of Science*, vol. 48, pp. 19–49.

Layton, E. (1977), 'Conditions of technological development' in Spiegel-Rösing and de Solla Price (eds), op. cit., pp. 197–222.

Lenin, V. I. (1952), *What Is To Be Done?* (Moscow: Foreign Languages Publishing House).

Licklider, R. E. (1971), 'Policy scientists and nuclear weapons', in Horowitz (ed.), op. cit., pp. 272–95.

Liebow, E. (1967), *Tally's Corner* (Boston, Mass.: Little, Brown).

Lipset, S. M. (1982), 'The academic mind at the top', *Public Opinion Quarterly*, vol. 46, pp. 143–68.

Lipset, S. M., and Dobson, R. B. (1972), 'The intellectual as critic and rebel', *Daedalus*, vol. 101, pp. 137–98.

Lipsey, D. (1980), 'What do we think about the nuclear threat?', *New Society*, 25 September, pp. 603–6.

Lunn, H. (1983), 'Our "divine right to riches" challenged', *The Weekend Australian*, 28–29 May, p. 4.

Lydall, H. (1968), *The Structure of Earnings* (Oxford: Clarendon Press).

Martin, B. (1979), *The Bias of Science* (Canberra: Society for Social Responsibility in Science).

Marx, K. [1847] (1975), *The Poverty of Philosophy*, in K. Marx and F. Engels, *Collected Works* (New York: International Publishers).

Marx, K. [1867] (1976), *Capital*, Vol. 1 (Harmondsworth: Penguin).

Marx, K. [1849] (1977), 'Wage-labour and capital', in D. McLellan (ed.), *Karl Marx: Selected Writings* (London: Oxford University Press), pp. 248–68.

Mayntz, R. (1977), 'Sociology, value freedom, and the problems of political counselling', in Weiss (ed.), op. cit., pp. 55–65.

McConnell, G. (1966), *Private Power and American Democracy* (New York: Knopf).

McKeown, T. (1976), *The Modern Rise of Population* (London: Edward Arnold).

Medawar, C. (1979), *Insult or Injury?* (London: Social Audit).

Melville, A., and Johnson, C. (1983), *Cured to Death* (New York: Stein & Day).

Merton, R. K. (1957), 'Social structure and anomie', in *Social Theory and Social Structure* (New York: The Free Press, rev. edn), pp. 131–60.

Merton, R. K. (1973), *The Sociology of Science* (Chicago: University of Chicago Press).

Miliband, R. (1974), 'Politics and poverty', in D. Wedderburn (ed.), *Poverty, Inequality and Class Structure* (Cambridge: Cambridge University Press), pp. 183–96.

Mitchell, B. R. (1975), *European Historical Statistics 1750–1970* (London: Macmillan).

Moynihan, D. P. (1969), *Maximum Feasible Misunderstanding* (New York: The Free Press).

Mulkay, M. J. (1977), 'Sociology of the scientific research community', in Spiegel-Rösing and de Solla Price (eds), op. cit., pp. 93–148.

Mulkay, M. (1979a), 'Knowledge and utility', *Social Studies of Science*, vol. 9, pp. 63–80.

Mulkay, M. (1979b), *Science and the Sociology of Knowledge* (London: Allen & Unwin).

Myrdal, G. (1969), 'Challenge to affluence', in C. S. Heller (ed.), *Structured Social Inequality* (New York: Macmillan), pp. 138–43.

National Academy of Sciences/National Research Council (1968), *The Behavioural Sciences and the Federal Government*, no. 1680 (Washington, DC: National Academy of Sciences).

National Science Foundation (1969), *Knowledge into Action* (Washington, DC: US Government Printer).

Nickels, T. (1980), *Scientific Discovery, Logic and Rationality* (London: Reidel).

O'Connor, J. (1973), *The Fiscal Crisis of the State* (New York: St Martin's Press).

OECD Economic Outlook (1973), no. 13, July; (1974), no. 15, July; (1982), no. 32, December (Paris: OECD).

OECD Economic Outlook – Historical Statistics (1982), (Paris: OECD).

OECD Main Economic Indicators (1983), June (Paris: OECD).

Parkin, F. (1979), *Marxism and Class Theory* (London: Tavistock).

Passmore J. (1978), *Science and its Critics* (London: Duckworth).

Patton, M. Q., *et al.* (1977), 'In search of impact', in Weiss (ed.), op. cit., pp. 141–63.

Popper, K. R. (1957), *The Poverty of Historicism* (London: Routledge & Kegan Paul).

Popper, K. R. (1972), *Objective Knowledge* (Oxford: Clarendon).

Potts, D. (1983), 'The late renaissance of Keynesian economics', *The Australian*, 10 June, p. 9.

Preston, M. B. (1984), *The Politics of Bureaucratic Reform* (Urbana, Ill.: University of Illinois Press).

Proudhon, P. J. (1846), *Systeme des contradictions économiques ou: philosophie de la misère* (Paris: Guillaumin).

Putnam, H. (1975), *Mathematics, Matter and Method*, Vol. 1 (Cambridge: Cambridge University Press).

Rich, R. F. (1977), 'Uses of social sciences information by federal bureaucrats', in Weiss (ed.), op. cit., pp. 199–211.

Rose, R. (1979), 'Ungovernability', *Political Studies*, vol. 27, pp. 351–70.

Rossi, P. H. (1980), 'The presidential address', *American Sociological Review*, vol. 45, pp. 889–904.

Samuel, P. (1984), 'US braces for poison warfare terror assault', *The Australian*, 29 February, p. 7.

Samuelson, P. (1983), '20th century seer with a flawless track record', *The Weekend Australian*, 9–10 July, p. 16.

Sapolsky, H. M. (1977), 'Science, technology and military policy', in Spiegel-Rösing and de Solla Price (eds), op. cit., pp. 443–71.

Schimmel, E. M. (1964), 'The hazards of hospitalization', *Annals of Internal Medicine*, vol. 60, pp. 100–10.

Schmitter, P. C., and Lehmbruch, G. (eds) (1979), *Trends Toward Corporatist Intermediation* (Beverly Hills, Calif.: Sage).

Schroeder-Gudehus, B. (1977), 'Science, technology and foreign policy', in Spiegel-Rösing and de Solla Price (eds), op. cit., pp. 473–506.

Schultze, C. L. (1977), *The Public Use of Private Interest* (Washington, DC: The Brookings Institution).

Schwebel, M. (1982), 'Effects of the nuclear war threat on children and teenagers', *American Journal of Orthopsychiatry*, vol. 52, pp. 608–18.

Selinger, B. (1981), *Chemistry in the Market Place* (Canberra: Australian National University Press).

Shanon, R. (1975), 'Inequality in the distribution of personal income', in *Education, Inequality and Life Chances*, Vol. 1 (Paris: OECD), pp. 109–58.

Shapere, D. (1974), 'Discovery, rationality and progress in science', in K. Schaffner and R. S. Cohen (eds), *PSA 1972* (Dordrecht: Reidel), pp. 407–19.

Sharpe, L. J. (1977), 'The social scientist and policy making', in Weiss (ed.), op. cit., pp. 37–53.

Shapiro, S., Slone, D., Lewis, G. P., and Jick, H. (1971), 'Fatal drug reactions among medical inpatients', *Journal of the American Medical Association*, vol. 216, pp. 467–72.

Shils, E. (1972), 'Intellectuals and the center of society in the United States', in his *The Intellectuals and the Powers and Other Essays* (Chicago: University of Chicago Press), pp. 154–95.

Silverman, M., and Lee, P. R. (1974), *Pills, Profits and Politics* (Berkeley, Calif.: University of California Press).

Smark, P. (1982), 'Jobless: a crisis here to stay', *The Age*, 9 August, p. 8.

Spiegel-Rösing, I., and de Solla Price, D. (eds) (1977), *Science, Technology and Society* (London: Sage).

Sydney Morning Herald, The (1982), 25 October, p. 7.

Toffler, A. (1970), *Future Shock* (New York: Random House).

Toffler, A. (1980), *The Third Wave* (London: Collins).

Toulmin, S. (1972), *Human Understanding* (London: Oxford University Press).

Touraine, A. (1971), *The Post Industrial Society*, trans L. F. X. Mayhem (New York: Random House).

Uliassi, P. D. (1971), 'Government sponsored research on international and foreign affairs', in Horowitz (ed.), op. cit., pp. 309–42.

United Nations (1949), *Demographic Yearbook 1948* (Lake Success, NY: UN).

United States Bureau of the Census (1976), *The Statistical History of the United States* (New York: Basic Books).

United States Bureau of the Census (1980), *Social Indicators* (Washington, DC: US Government Printer).

United States Bureau of the Census (1980, 1983), *Statistical Abstract of the United States* (Washington, DC: US Government Printer).

United States House of Representatives, Senate Sub-Committee on Government Operations (1967), *The Use of Social Sciences in Federal Domestic Programs* (Washington, DC: US Government Printer).

Useem, M. (1976), 'State production of social knowledge', American Sociological Review, vol. 4, pp. 613–29.

Weeramantry, C. G. (1983), *The Slumbering Sentinels* (Melbourne: Penguin).

Weekend Australian (1983), 16–17 July.

Weingart, P. (1974), 'On a sociological theory of scientific change', in R. Whitley (ed.), *Social Processes of Scientific Development* (London: Routledge & Kegan Paul), pp. 45–68.

Weiss, C. H. (ed.) (1977), *Using Social Research in Public Policy Making* (Lexington, Mass.: Lexington Books).

Westergaard, J., and Resler, H. (1976), *Class in Capitalist Society* (Harmondsworth: Penguin).

Wildavsky, A. (1973), 'Government and the people', *Commentary*, vol. 56, pp. 25–32.

Withers, G. (1978), 'The state of economics', *The Australian Quarterly*, vol. 50, December, pp. 74–80.

Withers, G. (1984), 'The arts applied to economics', proceedings of the Third International Conference on Cultural Economics, Ohio, April.

World Bank (1978), *The World Development Report* (Washington, DC: World Bank).

World Health Organization (1981), *World Health Statistics Annual 1981* (Geneva: WHO).

Wright, E. O., Hachen, D., Costello, S., and Sprague, J. (1982), 'The American class structure', *American Sociological Review*, vol. 47, pp. 709–26.

Yanarella, E. J. (1975), 'The technological imperative and the strategic arms race', *Peace and Change*, vol. 3, pp. 3–16.

Index

DATE DUE
DATE DE RETOUR

APR 1 4 1989			
JAN 0 4 1989			
DEC 0 9 1998			